BROKEN PROMISES

Joseph Lino Abyei

A Note from the Publisher

The publisher wishes to acknowledge and thank Dr Douglas H. Johnson for his invaluable help and support for Africa World Books and its mission of preserving and promoting African cultural and literary traditions and history. Dr Johnson and fellow historians have been instrumental in ensuring that African people remain connected to their past and their identity. Africa World Books is proud to carry on this mission.

© Joseph Lino Abyei, 2021

ISBN: 978-0-6450102-1-3

All rights reserved

No part of this publication may be reproduced, stored in a retrieval system, or transmitted, in any form, or by any means, electronic, mechanical, photocopying, recording or otherwise, without the prior permission of the publishers.

This book is sold subject to the conditions that it shall not, by way of trade or otherwise, be lent, re-sold, hired out or otherwise circulated without the publisher's prior consent in any form of binding or cover other than in which it is published and without a similar condition including the condition being imposed on the subsequent purchaser.

Cover design, typesetting and layout: Africa World Books
Cover image: Freepik

DEDICATION

This story is dedicated to the living memory of late Padre Domenico Muorwel Malow, preacher of the word of God and freedom fighter.

To the living memory of late Father Saturnino O'hure Hilange who fought the fight. He paid the price of liberty on Sudan-Uganda border at the hands of Sudan-Uganda security organs.

To the souls of all Anya-nya freedom fighters whose memory shall live forever.

CHAPTER ONE

Hot Autumn

This colonial official decided to withdraw from a memorial service that was underway in the Commonwealth Cemetery just across the railroad, not more than four hundred yards from here to go and capture an emergency meeting of the Council of Ministers of independent Sudan, scheduled to start about this time and date Monday August 29, 1955. Before he could cross the railway, the official stopped to allow a train carrying the last British contingent and members of their families to pass heading north, to Egypt and to other parts of Her Majesty's vast empire.

As he approached the compound of the new Council of Ministers, the colonial official found the outer compound walls all painted white. Approaching the entrance, the colonial official took note of some twenty or so prisoners, the majority of whom were black, working hard to clean up the surrounding area.

Before entering the compound of the Council of Ministers, the British official caught sight of Member of Parliament Dominic Muorwel Malow briskly walking along the street. Dominic, a former Roman Catholic priest, who resigned from the priesthood and joined politics the previous year thinking that by winning the election he would be able to represent his people in Parliament and make a difference. He was well educated and energetic, and he thought he was a committed politician as he was a priest, and he also believed that having principles and a good cause to fight for were enough to carry him through. Hence, MP Padre Domenico strongly believed that since the issue was this clear, all that was needed was proper articulation and forceful demand and the Arabs would acknowledge the right of the people of Southern Sudan for separation, if not, federalism would be acceptable.

In front of the premises of the Council of Ministers, the two men greeted each other, and the British colonial official explained that he was here to capture the first session of the first Council of Ministers. On his part, Dominic explained that he had come to check the dental hospital on the other side of the wall but found it closed, and that he was on his way home. "Why don't you wait and see what is going on?" the colonial official suggested.

Dominic: Noooo, no, no, no please, no.

The official: Why, don't you want to satisfy your curiosity, eh?

Dominic: No, no I see nothing interesting in all this.

The official: Any news from the South, of late, eh?

Dominic: I have not heard anything, so far.

The official: The rebels seem determined...

Dominic: It is a serious problem, and if...

The official: Oh yes, if...

Dominic: Well; it may become serious.

The official: Tell me who could be behind, I mean politicians, rebel leaders.

Dominic: Frankly, I have no idea. I have no idea at all.

The official: Well, I hope to see you on the issue, soon?

Dominic: I shall be pleased to see you, goodbye sir.

"Goodbye; stubborn we shall see," murmured the colonial official. Left standing alone, this last British official, so obedient to his profession, standing under the verandah newly painted white, observing the guards of honor and the military music band lined up under the neem trees not far from the entrance into the premises of the Council of Ministers. This last colonial official took note that all the tree trunks in the compound and those outside the compound of the Council of Ministers lining the newly asphalted street, were whitewashed.

The white man also noticed that the guards of honor were in their new neatly pressed khaki uniforms and shining boots, yet each one of them looked different from the other; some were short and bulky, others are slim and tall or lean and short, others had lighter complexion although the majority of them were black in color; "See how different they are; this is a new order, a new country," murmured this last colonial. The British official felt it was time for the Council of Ministers to convene.

The fifteen newly appointed ministers of this transitional cabinet represented the coalition government, but incidentally reflected certain regions of post-independent Sudan. As such the shapes, sizes and complexions of these ministers reflected the temperament and diversity of this vast country, thought this last departing British colonial official.

Standing here upright under the verandah, the last colonial official responded to a hand-wave, a greeting and exchanged smiles with some of the ministers passing by; some he knew, others he did not. In fact, this official standing upright watching and observing is Mr. Nigel Crawford, the Chief of the Intelligence soon to depart.

Overhearing what he initially thought was some noise while moving up and down under the verandah, Nigel Crawford soon understood it was some national song being played over the loudspeaker of the new mobile cinema van recently brought from Egypt for the occasion, approaching the premises of the Council of Ministers. Soon the van entered the compound and this Briton watched and listened as the sound blared so loud. The crew hurriedly alighted from the van and began to prepare to capture this historic occasion both in sound and picture; this is a new technology, and this is all under the background music of national songs such as:

Hey stranger, pack and go back to your country,
Pack your luggage, and pick your son,
Hey stranger, go back to your country...etc

This national song and others were played over and over. Suddenly the Egyptian head technician yelled at this slim young man to hurry up, "Shummu son, take those cables over there...come on, hurry boy, there is no time..." and this skinny young man, Ali Shummu, with his small sharp ears, scurried around to complete preparations before the entourage of the Prime Minister arrived.

Mr. Nigel Crawford caught sight of a small Irish woman on the second floor, briskly popping out from one office to another holding files and sheets of paper. Janet is the last personal secretary who Crawford personally introduced a few weeks ago to help the interim prime minister with secretarial work. She is very efficient, and now is very busy preparing to type and file documents of these last moments of her stay in this country as secretary; what a moment and what an assignment.

The sun was dull behind a screen of dust, waiting to fade away, as the wind began to blow away traces of the heavy sandstorm of the last night. Amidst all these preparations, two men in white prison uniforms carrying long brooms slowly shuffled around clearing the fallen leaves in the compound. The two men approached the white man from two different directions. They stopped and smiled at each other, said something in broken Arabic and then moved off in different directions. This white man discerned that these two are from Southern Sudan, "Poor fellows, it's too late. In the future you will either have it all, or none." He cast his head down to reflect on their situation. "Anyway, what future awaits them, why did they do it that way?" The last British Chief of the Intelligence enquired blowing away a lingering fly from his nose while shaking his small greyish hair.

The members of the newly appointed cabinet started to arrive, each in a different dress and style. Some were in the traditional long, flowing robe known as eiebaya with a turban wound around their heads, and another one around their necks. Some of them wore sandals made of leopard skin which is an indication of a high social position and dignity. Others were in Western straitjackets and neckties. Others were dressed in jellabiya without turbans, and others were wearing trousers and shirts; one minister was without a necktie. To this British security official, who happened to pass by on this hot dusty morning, whether on purpose or not, it was an amusing spectacle worthy of note. The departing British official also observed tension among these new ministers and noted that there was not a single Southern Sudanese among them except for the two men still sweeping the compound; what a gathering!

Very soon, the Council of Ministers shall hold an extraordinary session to review the security situation in the country with a particular emphasis on the South. Absent is Sir James Robertson, the Civil Secretary, Mr. Choudery, the Pakistani Attorney General, and the three South ern ministers. The agenda was distributed, and the ministers began to read from the sheets, others took notes. Faces were grim.

The Prime Minister called for attention and briefed the Council about the matters in hand. Although the three South ern ministers were absent the quorum was held, and the Council was officially in session. The Prime Minister read out the agenda of the day and asked for any remarks or observations.

Although proceedings in the Council of Ministers were in Arabic, large parts were conducted in English as well especially the technical aspects; laws and ordinances were still in English, high schools were taught in English, the medical profession was still in English, foreign relations were conducted entirely in English and the banking system was in English. The British and the Egyptian masters were preparing to depart finally, and Sudan shall soon be completely free, and there will be no more English language to disturb the Arab tongue.

Prime Minister: Gentlemen, I call upon the Minister of the Interior to brief the Council on the latest security situation in the country, I mean in the South of Sudan.

The minister rocked in this new chair, readying himself to speak. He picked up his papers, checked they were in order, adjusted his turban gently and began to read in a somewhat strained low voice, breathing heavily through his words. As he gathered momentum, his voice cleared although it was punctuated with heavy sighs indicative of the gravity of the situation. The minister assured the Council that all is well since the departure of the colonial administrators except in the Southern provinces. The minister assured the Council that intelligence assured of an underground movement whose aim is to separate the South speared headed by some students of Rumbek Secondary School nicknamed the Burning Spear who distributed leaflets which contained abusive language on the northerners whom they referred to as, "jellaba neo-colonizers, and he quoted a paragraph written in English:

> *Compatriots, we have dedicated ourselves to the cause of liberation from these neo-colonizers. We the Burning Spear call upon the true sons of the South to rise against the neo-colonizers…*
> *Long live…*

The minister paused, then highlighted the unrest in Anzara, which he termed as a local communist masterminded conspiracy which was brought down with minimum casualties, then continued:

> *Your Excellency the Prime Minister, my brothers, the ministers, another thing to be noted seriously is that South Sudanese government officials have*

been observed to abstain from socializing with their northern colleagues. They confine themselves either in their clubs or stay at home. This has made northerners to reciprocate by confining themselves to their clubs and homes.

The minister continued is his briefing reminding that "soon the British are going to depart once and for all insha Allah, and we shall see that Southerners should clear their minds of any prejudices they may have towards us instilled in them by the colonizers and the Church."

Having finished, the minister unwound his large turban which had fallen off his head during his speech, collected his reading glasses and his papers. The minister looked more agitated than when he began.

The Prime Minister of the caretaker government was short with a round head, a round face and a round belly. He was heavily built and with the tie his neck became much shorter and thicker. He was obviously over fifty years old and was known for humor as well as for wits.

The Prime Minister took time to look around the room, smiled and rocked from side to side, then started to speak in a rather thin voice while leaning against the table, those small round eyes bulging out behind the reading glasses; he mentioned that the report of the Minister of the Interior was comprehensive from a man who can be called an expert, and mentioned that, "As we near the end of the colonial days and hoist the flag of our dear country, we can claim that the country is so far enjoying peace and tranquility. This indicates to me that we're on the right path and, shall remain so, insha Allah."

Then he rocked from side to side on this new large smooth artificial black leather chair and continued touching on the security situation in the South and informed his colleagues that "time is appropriate to discuss such issues in the absence of these three ministers from the South," ministers Alfred Wani, David Angundit and Baluong, and continued:

> *In fact, I have two aims in mind; First, I want them out of this session; if you have something serious to do, better do it effectively. It is true that people like Alfred and Ba'alwang are innocent, but you can never know, and especially Alfred (Wagging his index finger at one of the three empty chairs.)*

The Prime Minister mentioned that he had a plan if they agreed with him "will nib all our troubles in the South in the bud, and the next generations will live in total peace in this country." He stopped to feel the effect of his words. Before he could resume talking, Mr. El Tijani, the Minister of Local Government, interrupted and asked to be briefed on the plan. As the Prime Minister prepared to answer, Mr. Mubarak, the Minister of Education, lit a cigarette and blew the smoke towards the ceiling.

Prime Minister: Well, as a matter of fact, it is an idea I have in mind for some time. If you insist, I'm ready to brief you on it; or I may put it down in writing, if there is no any objection eh, (All agree.)

The Prime Minister reached out for this new writing pad and pulled out his new fountain pen from the pocket of his new white shirt under his new white jacket offered to him by the new Egyptian Ambassador. This fountain pen, a new invention he was told, was given to him by a departing British friend. He is now using it officially for the first time. This is a new era, and this is a new country. This is a new cabinet, and this is a new government. These are new ministers, and they are all here in this new hall to handle this new but serious situation. The Prime Minister adjusted his new necktie and the new reading glasses and held this new pen tightly and began to write.

In the meantime, two other ministers opened their new brand cigarette boxes and pulled out two sticks and lit them up and smoke was becoming thick in the hall and this seemed to make El Tijani somewhat uncomfortable. Nevertheless, "ahemm, ehem let me see," the Prime Minister started while shaking his small round head from side to side. He cleared his throat again and after a short period of reflection he started to write while spelling out each sentence and each idea loudly:

> *After restoration of peace and tranquility in the South (The Prime Minister is bending to write in such a way that made the new chair to creak under him) all the officers in the armed forces, the police, the prison forces, and the games shall be transferred to the North immediately. Also, all government civil servants shall be transferred to the North and relocated in various towns in the North and this shall include teachers and senior civil servants for the purpose of training.*

Having finished writing, he put the pen down, then took off his glasses, placed them slowly on the table and beamed at the ministers with a radiant face, a face they have never seen before. This is a new face of a new prime minister of a new country, but what a face! "What do you think, eh?"

"Excellent indeed, Your Excellency," snapped El Tijani.

The Minister of the Interior expressed admiration that the Prime Minister has a very good command of the language and then addressed his colleagues in a serious manner that the Prime Minister has not given them any chance to add a dot, then added that, "I think if this statement is adopted into policy, it will put an end to our future problems with those people," the Minister concluded pointing towards the South. Then a short interlude of informal discussion followed.

In their new white uniforms, the newly appointed Halfawi caterers rushed to serve tea and coffee under the stern eyes of their old Egyptian butler, who was particular about his long years of service, and his long thick mustache which he carefully kept stroking. More cold water was supplied and served in new glasses on exquisite new trays. And then, a cup of coffee dropped from the shivering hand of this young caterer and coffee spilled over the tablecloth; Oh, Atta Allah, the Egyptian butler, got mad with the boy. He apologized to the ministers in the traditional Egyptian accent and style and begged them to allow the tablecloth to be removed and a new one brought, "Hey boy hurry, hurry son, I say hurry up," he is furious, apologetic, and agitated at the same time, and his long mustache turned up in rage against this shivering boy.

The Egyptian checked if the minister got any stain of the coffee and the minister assured him that there was nothing "Atta Allah, it is okay, okay. No there is nothing I am okay Atta, Atta don't worry" the minister kept assuring the Egyptian that his clothes were clean while the Egyptian butler fumed at the boy and at the same time broadly smiled to appease this minister and the rest of the ministers, a trademark that he is a seasoned butler and a true Egyptian highly conscious of his job.

The shivering boy brought the new tablecloth, and all the caterers came in timidly together to place it on the table. At last, the Egyptian, theatrically, and politely called upon the ministers to resume their session amid apology after apology with a promise to teach the boy a lesson he shall never forget. At this, all the ministers including the Prime Minister were much more amused than upset. This incident came as a sort of relief.

The Prime Minister made some remarks on this small incident recalling a similar one involving him while in Egypt, and the Council roared with laughter. This incident had become a chance for a change in atmosphere. Such incidents do happen.

The episode over, the Council resumed the meeting, and the Minister of Local Government was the last to speak.

Minister of Local Governments: I hope that they won't make problems to us especially if they know that it is government policy.

Prime Minister: No, no they won't. But if they do, they will not forget it for the rest of their lives. And mind you (Pointing at the Minister of the Interior) this is your duty.

Minister of Interior: Of course, of course Your Excellency (Smiling) No, rest assured, I will see that security is not tampered with anywhere, anytime, nor by anyone.

Minister of Labor: Gentlemen, may I say something.

Prime Minister: Go ahead.

Minister of Labor: I think that we have to consolidate

the government's presence in that part of the country by sending more forces, and more staff. Of course, this is in line with the policy of the Prime Minister, I think.

Minister of Local Governments: May I have your permission, sir. It is in the context of the Prime Minister's statement. I would like to say that my colleague, the Minister of Labor, has just mentioned a very important point. He suggested, if I have understood him well, that more staff be sent down to the South as a matter of urgency to execute the government policy requirements. This is sound. But the problem is where do we get those willing to go to the South, especially after these sad events.

Prime Minister: I think that the apprehension of the Minister of Local Governments is in place. But we need a plan or a policy, you may call it so, that encourages our employees to go to the South. For instance, there could be an incentive, a special allowance. This is our opportunity to talk and plan freely before those of Wani could come back.

Minister of Local Governments: I agree with you, sir. I think we shall stick to the book when time comes. Besides, new regulations and rules will have to be devised so that transfers are carried out because we need more people to go to the South. The South is of vital importance to us.

Minister of Education: I think a system of incentives can be devised so more of my men will be encouraged to go to the South.

Prime Minister: Wonderful. I think we are coming closer to the basic point. (He paused and continued) We all seem to agree on the gist of the matter that the situation in the South could escalate. But if this statement takes shape into policy, it will be the iron fist and the safety valve against any possible future subversion besides, South Sudan is not only a Sudanese territory, it is an extension of the Arab nation deep into black Africa and, as you know, Africa is starting to emerge from colonialism and will need the invigorating Arab power soon, then he continued, "Gentlemen, we cannot acquiesce on the South because it is a historic trust, and we are duty bound to keep the trust. For in South Sudan lies our future as a state not to forget the Arab world and the Islamic world too, just think of that."

The room was deadly quiet except the buzzing of the fans. The Prime Minister continued:

> *Gentlemen, I think everything has become clear to you now. However, what I want from you is the spirit of this message as a policy over the South at least to cover this crucial transitional period. What we need at this stage is action not words. We should not give any impression, especially to the British, that we can compromise, and you have just seen one of them standing under the verandah.*

The Prime Minister paused and picked up a note passed to him by the Minister of the Information and Social Affairs. He adjusted his glasses to read the note silently, and then continued:

> *One additional important point if executed would help us to establish our roots firmly in the South. This way we shall secure the integrity of this country. Moreover, it will allow the young generations in the South to have an insight into Arabic and Islamic culture and we will be able to establish a sound basis for future stability for this country.*

With a heavy sigh, the Prime Minister stopped, took off his glasses and then leaned back. The ministers, apparently impressed, began to exchange glances of satisfaction, except the Minister of Defense who seemed busy over his notes. The Minister of Education asked for a permission to speak.

As Minister of Education, he must sound as impressive as possible because Arabic is a matter of eloquence, and the more eloquent you are, the more highly regarded you are, reason and logic follow. The minister started that the Council had listened to an impressive speech from the Prime Minister and would go along with it "to ensure stability in that part of the country," and thought that "a stable country is not built on security measures alone."

In his speech, the Minister of Education mentioned that the Prime Minister had struck an important chord when he touched upon the cultural aspects of the matter, and suggested the takeover of all the Missionary Schools, and suggested a change of the pattern of education and the curriculum in the South, "for we cannot, or should not have two patterns of education in the same country," and further suggested that English be abolished from the schools in the South and Arabic introduced. This way, the minister thought, "we will remove a cause of misunderstanding in the future," and that "Arabic language and culture will be infused into the Africans of the Sudan like in Darfur and other parts of the country."

The suggestions won approval as seen from those twinkling eyes and those broad smiles. At this junction, the minister of Local Governments took permission to speak and mentioned that the cultural policy over the South and other parts of the country, and that "Islam has a much greater chance to spread in South Sudan and in the whole of black Africa, truly, I say if given chance." The minister begged to borrow the words of his colleague, the Minister of Education that, "Arabic language and culture, and may I add that Islam, will be infused into the African peoples of the Sudan and possibly the rest of black Africa."

Prime Minister: (With a broad smile) Gentlemen, this is a serious matter. What you are saying is becoming more interesting and more practical. This is what we are after. We would like to see South Sudan, which has suffered isolation for so long because of colonialism, is re-absorbed into the Sudanese mainstream society gently but firmly and decisively. It is our duty to see that is done."

Omer El Kurdi, the Minister of Defense, had been quietly but keenly following the deliberations, and diligently taking notes. The Prime Minister looked at El Kurdi and then called for the attention. He introduced the Minister of Defense to speak on the security situation in the South. It was no secret that the Prime Minister and his defense minister were close. The Prime Minister believed El Kurdi was needed for such a post and especially when this new country is at the threshold of independence and was facing a threat.

Moreover, the small new Sudanese Defense Force needed more units, more training and new weapons and equipment urgently. All this required an able man. Besides, El Kurdi was that type of a man who could be called a toughminded no-nonsense man. Having been introduced, El Kurdi who mentioned that he considered himself lucky to be a member of this cabinet and to serve under His Excellency the Prime Minister, a man who dedicated himself to the wellbeing of this new state and, above all, a man who was dedicated to the cause of 'Aoruoba'.

The cabinet was deadly quiet, and all eyes were fixed on this big figure with a broad chest, a broad face, a broad forehead, and broad palms. The minister continued and mentioned that he would confine himself to the question of security and its implications which he considered to be the topic of the hour. Then he went on to elaborate on all the steps he will take to ensure that no any mutiny shall ever take place again in that part of the country emphasizing his strong views on the student politics that:

> *But students are always a source of trouble. To deal with them, initially, we shall give the Minister of the Interior a freer hand. And should they continue to cause trouble we won't hesitate to come in. In fact, it will be our pleasure to use the language they best understand. We should not allow terroristic groups like the Burning Spear to exist. Of course, I am saying this in the hope that all shall be well.*

In the end the minister promised that he will teach the mutineers a lesson they will never forget, and that any slight movement, underground or not will be crushed immediately and without any mercy wiping the table with his large thick left palm to demonstrate what he meant, his large protruding eyes betrayed hatred and anger. He further unfolded the blueprint of his plans to mobilize the army, and prospective targets, and expressed his support for the Prime Minister's plan because "it is a very important step at this crucial stage in the life of this young nation." The minister voiced his support for the idea of incentives to encourage the northern Sudanese staff to go to the South.

With that, he threw the notebook on the table and took in a deep breath, then leaned back to calm himself down. The newly fixed fans are whirling faster as heat soared as it had been for a week or so since the last rain.

The cabinet continued in session and nearly everyone had expressed an opinion on the security situation in the South. The Prime Minister called for attention and expressed satisfaction over El Kurdi's clear plans. He looked around for further comments. Like the rest of the other ministers Mr. Abdel Jalil Abu Ali, the new Minister of Justice, a tall man of forty-five years or so, came in to clarify certain points of constitutional ambiguity and those of legal conflict. This responsibility was usually carried out by Mr. Chaudhry the Attorney General who was absent.

Before he could speak the Minister of Justice threw his

long white turban carelessly round his shoulders to free his head for more fresh air, exposing his bushy unattended hair which he kept scratching. He stroked his mustache several times as he prepared to talk. He started with a brief commentary on the significance of the Prime Minister's policy, seeing nothing legally wrong with it since it will be an act of sovereignty. He lauded the incentive plan to encourage certain sectors of the civil service to go to the South in view of the absence of qualified local civil servants.

However, the minister stressed that "Let's not forget we have a democratically elected Constituent Assembly, and it represents different interests and shades of opinion, and this includes the South besides, we have a free Press and we have to put all this into consideration."

Mr. Sulieman Abubakr, the Minister of Information and Social Affairs, asked whether the resolutions of the cabinet shall be taken to the Constituent Assembly for ratification.

Minister of Justice: This is not necessary constitutionally speaking. Still, I am going to consult with Mr. Chaudhry but, in my opinion, since the country is facing an emergency, the government is empowered by the transitional constitution to take extra-emergency measures, and to execute them without recourse to the Assembly.

Minister of Defense: I was going to resign immediately if you had not clarified that point in that way. I cannot tolerate such a thing.

Minister of Local Governments: Easy, easy gentlemen.

Minister of Defense: There is no patience and there is no time to waste while the mutineers are still out there causing trouble.

Another interlude of discussion ensued, and all the points raised were adopted as resolutions. The Minister of Justice assured the cabinet further that their resolutions are in place and dispelled fears of any future constitutional complications and asserted the right of this young state to exercise its sovereignty. He further reiterated the fact that these resolutions do not need ratification from the Constituent Assembly and concluded that "the Attorney General's Chamber will have to put all these things into their legal frame."

Minister of Local Governments: Again, have we not just finished with this point, just now or what, aah?

Prime Minister: There is nothing called 'again,' (The cabinet roared with laughter and the Prime Minister continued with some humor) These are normal steps usually taken in any country isn't it or what, aah?" (Addressing himself to the Minister of Justice and the Council.)

Minister of Education: We have still a lot to learn (He said this in English while looking around from face to face.)

Prime Minister: (In English with some humor) There will be a lot to learn, but let me remind you of our resolutions, gentlemen. (Then he reads out the resolutions in Arabic slowly and in a clear voice:

1. The August Council has resolved that Mr. Ismail Al Azhari, the Prime Minister, Mr. Omer El Kurdi, the Minister of Defense, and Mr. Abdel Azim Tayifur, the Minister of the Interior, urgently seek audience with HE Sir Alexander Knox Helm, the Governor General to discuss with him the sad news coming from the South.
2. To seek urgent assistance from the Co-Domini Administration to re-establish law and order in the South.
3. To seek urgent military and economic assistance from the Government of Her Majesty for the Government and people of the Sudan.

The cabinet continued to deal with other matters concerning a proposal to levy new taxes to cover the impending expenditure on war activities in the South. There were other proposals that called for building five new secondary schools and a few new hospitals in various towns of the Sudan. But more importantly the cabinet passed a resolution to revive a pre-independence plan to extend the railroad to Wau in South Sudan.

It was now late in the afternoon when the cabinet wound up. The Prime Minister got up and wobbled out of the room followed by the rest of the ministers. They all sat in the lounge for a while and more refreshments were served. It had been a long day.

CHAPTER TWO

Long Nose

Today dust has already cleared from the air over Khartoum although temperature remained high. Incidentally this hot weather seemed to coincide with the hot news that had arrived from the South, which inflamed passions in all the circles, the Northern Sudanese, the British colonial, and the Southern Sudanese circles.

Although people in the marketplace walked about calmly, yet tempers were high for newspapers kept reporting wild news from the South for days. Those who have family members there began to express worry. This, among others, prompted the Council of Ministers to hold the extra-ordinary meeting yesterday.

The session was a result of the fact that the government was shocked to the spine by the news of the mutiny, its magnitude, the alleged damage, and the reported loss of life it brought among the Northern Sudanese civilians residing in the South and, above all, the serious implications that the South had seceded.

As approved yesterday in the Council of Ministers, the Prime Minister Ismael Al Azhari sought audience with the Governor General Sir Alexander Knox Helm nine days after his arrival from his annual vacation which he spent on the mountains in Scotland.

On their way to the Palace, the Prime Minister was in his customary all white suit and a spotted blue necktie. Omer El Kurdi was in a dark blue safari suit while Tayifur was in a white garment and a long turban wound round his thin neck and flowing over his rather bony narrow shoulders.

At the gate of the Palace, a throng of the guards of honor saluted as their motorcade entered the compound of the Palace. Waiting down the steps of the Palace was Mr. J. Jones, Secretary of the Governor General.

The Governor General was waiting, he is slightly over sixty years old and although his hair is covered with some white hair, he looked physically fit. Moreover, he had a long sharp nose, piercing blue eyes glittering behind those rimless reading glasses. His face was covered with smooth whiskers. With him is Sir James Robertson, the outgoing Civil Secretary who, until a few weeks ago, was the acting Prime Minister of the Sudan.

As the Prime Minister and his delegation approached the door, Sir Alexander Knox Helm put the file from which he was reading a report on the table and walked to meet his guests, his arms wide open, while smiling gently. Sir James stood to receive the Prime Minister and his delegation, and they all shook hands vigorously. With his habitual humor, the interim Prime Minister greeted the Governor General warmly then Sir Robertson. Sir Robertson introduced the delegation:

Sir Robertson: Governor General, this is the interim prime minister and his delegation (Smiling big.)

Prime Minister: How do you do, Sir? (Doing his best to sound as British as possible at the background of his heavy Arab accent.)

Governor General: Well indeed and you, Sir?

Prime Minister: I'm, in fact, *we* are very well, Sir.

The interim prime minister turned around to introduce his colleagues, a habit which is not typically Sudanese.

Prime Minister: This is Sayyid Omer El Kurdi. He is our new Defense Minister, and he is a very capable man as you can see, Sir.

Governor General: Oh yes, I can see. (Nodding his grey head several times.)

Prime Minister: This is Sayyid Abdel Azim Tayifur. Tayifur is the new Minister of the Interior. I fully trust him just like you do in England, eh.

Governor General: Indeed, I see, very well. Welcome gentlemen. You're most welcome.

While all are still standing, the Governor General looked around to check things, then continued "Well gentlemen, be seated (He then continued) I'm delighted to see you Mr. Prime Minister. It has been quite a time since we last met. I hope that all of you are well."

The Prime Minister humorously answered affirmatively while broadly smiling and laughing as usual. Then he found a chance to ask about conditions in London.

Governor General: Oh, London was unusually warm for this time of the year, or should I say hot. It reminded me of Kaatuum rather, you know.

Prime Minister: Sudan is always warm, even in winter, Your Excellency (Small laughter.)

Minister of Interior: It is said also that the people of the Sudan are warm (A large grin.)

Governor General: Oh yes.

Sir Robertson: It's true; the Sudanese are a very warm people in terms of generosity, I mean you know (A large grin.)

Governor General: Gentlemen, time for refreshments; tea, coffee, the new soft drink called Coca Cola, or kharkhadeh perhaps? Kharkhadeh! what is kharkhadeh? (Turning to Sir James Robertson.)

Sir Robertson: Hibiscus.

Sir Knox Helm: Oh yes, hibiscus. I personally ask for hibiscus, I mean kharkhadeh; little sugar please. (Tayifur interceded to correct Sir Knox Helm.)

Tayifur: It is not kharkhadeh; it is karkade…karkade, you see.

Sir Knox Helm: Karkhadeh I see, best product of the Sudan, isn't it?

Tayifur: Correct, there is also ground nuts and sesame,

you see. Gum Arabic yes, cotton also. A lot of these products we have in the Sudan, you know.

Governor General: Yes, I see, I see (Nodding.)

Sir Robertson: Sudan is a typical agricultural country, you know.

They all commend karkade and the Sudanese in particular laud the Governor General for taking it and encouraged him to take more karkade "because it cleans the kidney, you see, and has lots of health benefits, you see," Tayifur elaborated.

Sir Robertson: Yes, that is true.

Refreshments were brought and served by Katta, an old Halfawi servant who had been in the Palace for years, in fact since the days of Sir, Francis Reginald Wingate. This man seemed sad; he was afraid perhaps he may be left behind in the cold when Sir Robertson finally leaves for another part of the world. Or perhaps he was not sure whether he will continue to receive the same kind treatment and privileges he and his family had been enjoying under the old order.

Katta could see the colorful fruits of independence dangling in the lustrous eyes of these fidgeting guests sitting in front of him. Katta and his fellow Halfawi servants here in the Palace and in the other houses of the departing British officials would spend hours debating the virtues of independence; some of them are for it, "…it is good to be free, let the khawajat go to their country; this is our country." Some of them were not so sure of their future under these people, while others expressed a desire to join Egypt "…because that is where our real roots are, and Egypt is well advanced, not like here," and "there is good education there, what do these people know," one of them would strongly argue. These Halfawis would argue touching on different political and social aspects of the impending independence whenever time permitted and independence was fast approaching, and here it is right in front of him reflected in these anxious eyes, "Thank you Katta," snapped the Governor General, and Katta quietly retreated.

As it overlooked the southern bank of the Blue Nile, the office of the Governor General was furnished rather modestly. There was nothing new. The curtains were not fashionable as they hang up there. The table of the Governor General and some smaller ones are made of local mahogany, but well-polished and they shined. The set of the armed chairs, the large two sofas and the carpets, though imported, are apparently not of expensive quality. There are three fresh flower bouquets in different locations in this spacious office. The table of the Governor General was medium in size, and there were two or three files on it and a telephone. The chairs were on a Turkish carpet that had covered the office. Of course, the walls were decorated with the photographs of this very young Queen standing alone, anther one is showing her with her parents. There is the portrait of General Charles Gordon and others depicting the London Bridge and the Westminster, in addition to other landmarks in England. The Governor General did not forget to hang the photographs of the confluence of the Nile and photos of other sites of interest in the Sudan.

Hanging from this high ceiling were two fans swirling to dispel this heat and the dust. Besides, there was plenty of light and fresh air flowing in through these high French-style windows that remind all the Governor Generals of the previous Turko-Egyptian occupation and hence the French traces. In general, the office was quite exquisite reflecting the dignity befitting a departing colonial Governor General. Some light discussion took place while Katta was still serving refreshments.

Sir Knox Helm: I have just been reading an article in The Guardian; it's analyzing political affairs in the Soviet Union. Interesting!

Sir Robertson: Reports on the Soviet Union are getting interesting these days.

Sir Knox Helm: I'm afraid pretty soon we're going to feel the weight of the growing Soviet hegemony and influence in many parts of the world. I think there is fear it's going to be an awfully dangerous world.

Al Azhari: I think Sir, that the Soviet Union will be a real threat to you and to the world very soon, if you are not careful.

Sir Knox Helm: Well, for that matter, the West will have to pull up its sleeves tightly high you know. (Then adds after a short reflection) Presently, I think we've enough power at our disposal to go by only how to use it, if I may say, is the concern.

Al Azhari: Exactly Sir, this is always the problem. One may have power but may not know how to use it to achieve his aims or objectives you see. This is why we are here Sir, to see you in your office today, Your Excellency.

The two ministers immediately checked up to prepare

for the topic for which they have come. Sir Alexander Knox Helm took out his pipe lit up to smoke, The British are attentive, especially Sir Helm. In the meantime, Al Azhari looked around at his colleagues to prop them up for the debate. After giving the Governor General time to pull his pipe, Al Azhari resumed his expose. The Prime Minister assumed an unusually serious manner and so were his colleagues. He opened his notebook and resumed talking while focusing his eyes on the Governor General and started by reminding about the security situation in the country, especially in the south of Sudan. He stopped to check his notes and the office is deadly quiet and all the British eyes are fixed on this round figure sitting at the edge of this large sofa facing the Governor General. The Prime Minister reminded the British that in 1952 England and Egypt agreed that Sudan and South Sudan should achieve impendence together, and that "…we agreed with our Southern brothers in Juba in 1947 that Sudan to be one and united," and that they are shocked by what has happened in the South. He stopped to reflect while still in a serious mood and his round face became rounder and there was no humor but was about to turn emotional. The other two faces were grim as never before.

The Prime Minister went on to elaborate on the seriousness, the magnitude, and the damage the mutiny in the South had caused, and that until that moment there was no communication with the South.

The Governor General, who had been listening in a composed manner, began to show signs of anxiety. He looked at Sir James Robertson trying to read his mind then fixed his sharp blue eyes on the Prime Minister.

The Prime Minister went on rambling that the situation should not be allowed to go on like that, and that if the mutineers "…are left to do things in the way they like, we will soon say goodbye to Sudan," and that the situation may adversely affect the neighboring British possessions, and that there is fear Russia may get involved because "we think this mutiny is communist masterminded." Then the Prime Minister asked, "Her Majesty's government to help to restore sovereignty, and that "…we want you to promise assistance to our government in future similar situations also."

Having finished, the Prime Minister pulled his heavy body back into the sofa. Before Sir Alexander Helm could speak Mr. Tayifur asked for permission to say a word elaborating on the points Mr. Al Azhari had already made.

Tayifur: Your Excellency, (Broadly smiling) the Prime Minister is very clear. The situation in the South can be said to be out of our control now. But we blame the communists and the separatists. Look at this paper Sir, it was distributed just two months before the mutiny, it is communist propaganda; it is very clear they speak of injustice and, and mistreatment and this is even before independence.

He handed the leaflet to the Governor General who gave it a quick look. Tayifur continued, "They have even infiltrated the students." He stopped to gasp and continued with eyes wide open:

> *That is why we have come to Your Excellency to put you in the picture, and and to ask you to do something to help the situation, otherwise our celebrations for independence may be spoiled, or delayed."*

Sir Helm: (He looked at Sir Robertson) I see.
Omer El Kurdi lurched forward raising his thick palm

demanding to speak. He spoke with no marked courtesy showing a sign of anxiety and discomfort. He mentioned that the mutiny started when we "were preparing to transfer some units of the Southern military to Khartoum so that they could take part in the independence parade, and that the order was misunderstood and some people took it to create problems, and emphasized saying that they will not rest until law and order are restored in the South of the Sudan, "by the will of Allah, and…and before Independence Day, insha Allah." He then pulled himself back into the seat, his eyes crimson.)

Sir Helm: Very well, (He is now feeling the gravity of the situation and he too is beginning to look grim, his small blue eyes becoming smaller and less blue) but tell me, Sir (Addressing Al Azhari) what is the nature of the message I heard you sent down to the South; don't you think Sir, that might have inflamed the situation?

Al Azhari: (He cleared his throat as he rocked from side to side trying to appear innocent by putting on a big smile. Tayifur shrank in size while El Kurdi appeared more nervous) myself, I am surprised. I have also heard that a message was sent from my office but (Still radiant with smile) I can assure you that no message or, or anything like that Sir, was sent out from my office.

The Minister of the Interior who was listening attentively could not wait for Al Azhari to end.

Tayifur: Your Excellency, (Extending his hand towards the Governor General begging for understanding) saboteurs can do anything, anything. The Prime Minister has not sent any message to, to the South at all.

Governor General: (Leaned back as if to distance himself from any implication and to ward off any commitment) I understand (In a calm but serious tone) that some MPs from the South are not happy over this. (Prime Minister's eyes suddenly get larger) Indeed, some of them attribute the current strife, if I may call it, to this message and the secret nature of your dealings with them, they say.

Al Azhari: (Pulled out his handkerchief to wipe out sweat from his face and round his short thick neck. The weather is getting hot here. Again, he rocked himself onto the edge of the sofa to make himself clearer while smiling big. He said that there was news that problems were taking place in the South, and that they want peace. He emphasized that this message was invented to undermine the government and maybe to spoil the good relations with Great Britain. After stopping for a while, the Prime Minister stressed:

> ...*how can we be secretive to our brothers in the South, we have consulted them on any matter ... on any matter, believe me.*

He went on to mention that a number of MPs from the Southern Sudan are in Political Parties in the North and they "discuss all matters with us frankly, no discrimination Sir, no."

Sir James Robertson: I beg your pardon Sir, (Addressing the Prime Minister) I understand that the three Southern representatives in your cabinet did not attend the last meeting of the Council of Ministers.

Al Azhari: (Looked perplexed and El Kurdi was more perturbed) Yes Sir; Alfred Wani told me that he was going to the South to check the situation and to report to me. This is very good. Mr. David was ill (Looking at Tayifur for confirmation) very ill, and I sent Othman El Shingaity to visit him in his house last week eeer and Mr. Ba'a, Ba, what ah? (Looks to Tayifur for the name) yes, Balwang you see, he travelled to Malakal to see the situation and then to report to me.

Tayifur: (Immediately interjected with anxiety clear on his face) Our fear is the result of the mutiny. We are afraid that such a movement may take place in Kenya or, or in, in Uganda.

Sir Robertson: Exactly Mr. Tayifur; that's one of the things that concern us the most.

Sir Helm: Speaking of the communist danger, I beg your pardon Sir, (Obviously addressing the Prime Minister and the rest in the office) do not underestimate that. The Soviet Union is an emerging superpower poised to exploit such situations.

Sir Robertson: That is awfully true, I think something has got to be done Sir, (Addressing Sir Knox Helm) to restore law and order in the South (Adds quickly focusing on the Sudanese) but be careful. Ordinary South Sudanese should feel that the operations are not directed against them or I'm afraid we're going to have similar uprisings in the future eh.

Al Azhari: Of course, of course Sir James. We shall be careful, the citizens of the South will not be touched, and their properties and their lives. I assure you very much Sir James, Sir Helm.

Sir Knox Helm: Well, gentlemen (He stops smoking and leans forward almost resting his chest on the table and looking straight into the eyes of the Sudanese one by one, and goes on stressing) You may know gentlemen, that Her Majesty's Government does not tolerate insurrections and mutinies for that matter. (He continues looking serious, his long nose pointing at each Sudanese in and out of the office) as well as it does not tolerate injustice either. May I remind you gentlemen, that injustice is the root cause of all troubles and evil deeds.

The office suddenly became so quiet the heavy sound of a landing airplane about two miles away was interfering. Al Azhari put his notebook aside to concentrate for it appeared to him that the fate of independent Sudan was being redetermined. Abdel Azim Tayifur quickly finished his coffee, and both ministers became much attentive. The Governor General continued and mentioned that he was greatly perturbed when he first heard the news over the BBC and was put under pressure by the Home Office and the Foreign Office for more credible information, and that he got instructions from Sir Anthony Eden personally and from the Secretary of the State to supply information; and continued:

> *Let me remind you gentlemen. It was decided in Juba in 1947, if I may recall, that the South and the North be reunited and work together towards independence, and that the North is charged with the responsibility to help the South to catch up you know; development, schools, and so on you know.*

He stopped to recollect. He looked at J. Jones to his left who was busy taking notes. He continued when J Jones stopped writing using the same measured tone. The hoot of a steamboat about fifty meters away in the Nile was heard in the office.

It is true that both South and North may be two distinct peoples, strictly my personal opinion gentlemen, but because of geography and certain other considerations you know, it was convenient to keep the South with the North united in a hope that both may help each other, you know, and develop together, as one country. I should make this point clearer to you gentlemen, nearly all the Southerners I have met felt cheated, this is the term they used over Sudanization for example. Some of them would go as far as to accuse the North of eeer eeer of 'domination' and this is very serious.

Al Azhari and his ministers remained silent and grim, for they did not expect this turn of the events, El Kurdi in particularly was irritated. The Sudanese delegation was apprehensive perhaps because such "sensitive" issues were being touched when independence was just a few months away, especially by a man like Alexander Knox Helm.

> *I'm not defending them mind you (Sir Helm is sounding apologetic) but only trying to highlight certain points of weakness in the Sudanese polity, I mean in the Sudanese society, you know....*

The Governor General went on to touch on many aspects of the "mutiny" and what it means to Her Majesty's government, and the implications of an independent South Sudan:

The most important points I want to make clear to you gentlemen, (The Governor General is preparing to conclude and looks at J Jones for attention in putting down the points) are as follows: First: we do stand by our commitment pledged in 1947 and similar subsequent declarations regarding the unity of this country, North and South, and its territorial integrity. Second: We strongly condemn the mutiny in the strongest terms, and Third: (Takes time to think over) yes, third; on behalf of Her Majesty's Government, I promise to offer any immediate assistance required to the caretaker government of the Sudan up to a degree to allow it to stand on its feet.

With that, Ismael Al Azhari and the two ministers expressed relief and began to feel relaxed, satisfied, and proud. To them the battle for independence had been re-won today and a great victory indeed had been achieved. It was a moment of immense happiness.

The Battle won and independence secured, everybody felt relaxed. The Governor General leaned back as if to withdraw his sharp long nose from the battlefield, his arms crossed over his stomach. Ismael Al Azhari, ever radiant with eagerness, took this opportunity to reveal the best of his political wits; he started: "Your Excellency, Your Excellency," looking into the face of the Governor General, life was vibrant in his big body and this big stomach was dancing with happiness, then continued and thank the Governor General on behalf of his colleagues for having restored confidence in them, and that the Governor General had given their struggle for independence a meaning.

The Prime Minister went on emotionally that it is true some Southerners have talked about injustice and fear of domination, and that this talk is not all true because it comes only from a small number of people, and that the majority of Southerners support unity with the North and that they did not cheat Southerners on Sudanization at all only because they did not have qualified people, and that their rights are well preserved and that they did not want to dominate anyone.

Sayyid Tayifur: Some Southerners accuse us of dominating them, this is not true at all, at all. For example, we regard Ali Abdel Latif as a true Sudanese nationalist, and he is from the South you see. He died for the sake of this country; you see. There are many Southerners like David Angundit who think Northerners and Southerners are brothers. The question of religion and language is not a problem at all at all. They are free in their religion, and they can speak their language also. You can see now, there is no domination at all, no?

Sir Robertson: Very well. But let's not forget that Juba Conference provided safeguards for the South until such a time they are fit enough to be on equal footing with the Sudanese. Only this way, Mr. Tayifur, you may avoid possible future disturbances if I may say.

Sir Knox Helm: Gentlemen, let's not forget, if you do not treat the problem of the South carefully and seriously, this may invite you lots and lots of problems with your neighbors and other international parties.

Omer El Kurdi: We totally agree with you, Sir. You have just assured us of your support to defeat the mutineers, and to restore peace to our country. We will work hard to see that another mutiny should not take place again, yes again.

Discussion seemed to heat up again while the Sudanese used all the skills, trying to strengthen their positions. As they exchanged views, Sir Alexander Knox Helm made a sign to say something, and they all stopped talking to listen:

Well gentlemen, I'm pleased to receive you, Mr. Prime Minister, Mr. El Kurdi, Mr. Tayifur. It has been a chance to exchange opinions. We feel satisfied that we have done our best towards the Sudanese. Britain has ruled Sudan as one country and as one country we're handing it over to you. (He stopped for a while to reflect, then continued) Fifty years ago, this country was a wasteland, almost you know. Looking back, we can say that something has been done; hundreds of miles of railways have been extended across the country and there is a plan to extend it to… Wau isn't it? (Looking at Sir James Robertson who nodded affirmatively) Now the rest is your responsibility; Gordon Memorial College will soon be turned into a university; I have been told. You have good; very good highways I suppose, and a workable river transport system. Your civil service is by now second to none in Africa far as I know. This is just to mention a few obvious examples. Gentlemen, bear in mind that such services and institutions do not exist in the South and I'm afraid to say that such institutions are lacking in many other British possessions. (The Governor General stopped for a while to survey the office and to reflect and then continued) Gentlemen, far as I know Southern Sudan was ruled on a care and maintenance basis; was it not like that Sir Robertson?

Sir Robertson: Yes Sir; fact was that conditions were backward in the South and there was nothing meaningful we could do to help the situation, and we thought of arranging things in such a way that we allowed the Jallaba to run the market, and the government to maintain law and order. Yeah, the Missionaries were allowed to run their schools and their churches, nothing more.

Sir Helm: Very good (He turned to the Sudanese directly) you have heard why the South has remained behind. From now on it is your responsibility to take care of it. (The office was as quiet a nighttime graveyard) Gentlemen, eer eer, when it was decided to re-unite the two parts; eer eer it was too late to eer eer start any meaningful development steps in that part of the country, you know, (Pointing towards the South.)

The Governor General looked at his notes. The Prime Minister and his two colleagues again were kept in suspense; what is happening, what does this man want to do? The Sudanese were wondering:

> *"Resting on what I have said, I must admit gentlemen, many Southerners have expressed reservations and may I remind you again, you're required to dispel their fears and their reservations. Her Majesty's Government will be watching and will lend you a helping hand whenever you ask.*

The Sudanese recomposed while the Governor General went on touching on many aspects of the problems of the Sudan and his experiences and predictions, stressing that if the Sudanese do not take grievances of the South into serious consideration, there will be a lot of trouble lying in store. The Governor General continued in the same trend of seriousness:

Regarding our pledge eer eer, we're going to take all the necessary steps to see tranquility prevails in the South; now the Prime Minister is given power to deal with the situation in the most appropriate manner. Sir Robertson and I will immediately inform the Foreign Office to standby with any required assistance we may need and, we have to notify Kenya and Uganda (Looking at Sir Robertson, then turned to the Sudanese focusing these two sharp blue eyes and this long nose on them) to close their borders with Sudan. Not to forget according to arrangements I and Sir Robertson will see you up to independence, after that Sir Robertson will leave for Nigeria. Immediately after 1st January; Chief Justice Mohamed Ahmed Aburanat will act as a caretaker Governor General to oversee the formation of the Sovereign Council of five members. Why Aburanat because he is nonpartisan. It is clear, isn't it? Gentlemen, I'm afraid our meeting seems to have come to an end; I wish you the best of luck.

With this nothing more needed to be added. This was

why the Sudanese came to see the Governor General. After a few minutes of socializing, the Sudanese asked to be allowed to leave and Sir Helm wished them well.

In less than four minutes, their brand-new cars arrived at the Council of Ministers. Sitting on his new Egyptian-style chair, Abdel Azim Tayifur lit up a cigarette, a bell was rung, and the errand boy rushed in and told to bring in plenty of tea, coffee, and cold water from the new fridge.

Tayifur: (After getting rid of his sandals, freeing his head from this long turban, and blowing thick smoke up towards the ceiling) What do you think of the khawajat, Omer?"

El Kurdi: Frankly I don't trust these people, nor do I like them. I have a feeling that Alexander is still sympathetic with the Janubiyeen but cannot do anything; I could see that, very strange!

Tayifur: Be fair with the man (The boy is serving tea) at least he has promised to help us deal with the mutiny. These instructions are from above, very high up I tell you, probably from Eden or maybe from the Queen herself. There is no joke about this.

El Kurdi: Have they any choice (The boy is careful to put a cup of coffee on the table by El Kurdi's side and moved away. El Kurdi reclined to one side to face Tayifur, while the Prime Minister was busy with his papers on the table) they came all the way from Europe to colonize us. I mean, they found us like this, and they must hand it back like this. If they fail, the Egyptians will give them a very hard time, you know, of course.

Al Azhari: I tend to agree with Abdel Azim because up to this point, I think the British have not let us down. At any rate, before we go ahead in this matter let us agree. (Stopped for a while scratching his head and looking here and there humorously. At this point the errand boy had left) I am suggesting that we meet somewhere sometime to review what has taken place today.

Tayifur: I agree, but why don't we meet on Friday night?

El Kurdi: Friday is too far. What about tonight? The mutineers won't wait for us.

Al Azhari: That is alright. Then let's meet at my house. But whom do you suggest coming?

El Kurdi: I suggest a very few people, one or two not more. Let us not give room for rumors.

Tayifur: You are really tough, Omer (Eyeing Omer intensely then continued) I am suggesting Mubarak Ahmed and, and possibly Othman El Shingaity.

El Kurdi: Othman El Shingaity!

Al Azhari: El Shingaity is a good young man. He is learned. (El Kurdi keeps quiet passing his hand over his head passively) Generally I agree with you Tayifur on your nominations. I am adding two more names from the party. It is necessary, you know.

They all agreed on the names suggested who will attend the meeting to be held this evening at the Prime Minister's residence overlooking the Nile in Omdurman. The office manager was instructed to make arrangements.

Another round of tea and coffee was served. Looking at his new watch the Minister of Defense asked for permission to leave for his office and permission was granted not after some insistence from the Prime Minister to stay for a while. Omer El Kurdi was soon followed by the Minister of the Interior heading for his office.

Before the Prime Minister could clear his mind of the problems of the day, his new secretary came in politely to tell him that a delegation from Kassala Province have been waiting to see him, and that a group of professors from the university of Khartoum would like to meet with him too.

He instructed the secretary to let in the Kassala delegation and make another appointment with the professors for tomorrow at 10 am. The rest of the afternoon was taken up by the meeting with this rather large delegation from Kassala which will be the evening news on the Radio and tomorrow's newspapers headlines.

CHAPTER THREE

Pleasant Night

The guests began to show up at about the appointed time at the residence of the Prime Minister. The last to arrive was Sayyid Othman Salih El Shingaity. As soon as he sat on the chair, a servant in new white robes and a green ribbon round his waist, immediately offered him a large glass of cold lemon juice. The Prime Minister emerged from one of the side rooms barefooted like the rest of his guests and entered the salon where they were seated. Close by was his four-year-old daughter Widad, whom the Prime Minister seemed to be fond of. He boisterously greeted the late arrivals in the usual Sudanese way of hugging and back-patting and introduced this nice-looking little girl dressed in a short dress. Dragging the girl along, he also vigorously shook hands with those he had greeted earlier amid "welcome, welcome your presence has illuminated the house, please be seated; Widad greet your uncles, these are your uncles eeh." Then he sat on a chair to join the company at the background of big smiles and laughter and Widad was fondly wedged between her father's legs and all eyes are fondly fixed on this cute little girl who speaks in Egyptian accent, for she was born in Cairo.

Before the Prime Minister could speak, Othman Salih El Shingaity observed the salon, sweeping his eyes from one end to the other expressing admiration, "such a saloon is rare to find in a country like this," he silently noted.

The salon is large and is well furnished by Sudanese standards. On one side is a complete set of Victorian furniture some people say is a gift from Sir James Robertson, a token of their long friendship. Opposite is a complete set of Egyptian furniture, also rumored to have been provided by the new Egyptian Ambassador. However, both sets have filled up the salon. There are other additional ordinary looking chairs fitted in between to provide maximum sitting space to accommodate all those who swarm in almost daily.

There are several rare paintings and photographs hanging against the four walls including a few academic credentials, and a bachelor's degree. In addition to all these pictures, are photographs of some Khitmiya religious sect leaders including a large photograph of the Prime Minister himself hanging against the wall. However, just close to the door hung the picture of the Queen and that of late King George VI and next to these photos is the picture of King Farouq of Egypt, Othman El Shingaity took note. There is a big radio at the far end of the salon whose big sound reaches this area of the salon.

Under the ceiling hung two large fans that provided fresh air in this warm weather in addition to two other mobile fans placed on the tables, "the salon is definitely very nice, very exquisite," El Shingaity said to himself. In the meantime, and after he had introduced Widad, the little nice-looking girl in rather short dress, is gently escorted out of the salon by Ismael Al Azhari into the interior part of the house. Resuming his seat, the Prime Minister pulled his new watch out from the upper pocket of his new large white jellabiya he is wearing this evening for ease of movement and more comfort. He made a sign to draw attention.

Al Azhari: Gentlemen (He slowly returned the watch into the small upper pocket of the jellabiya, smiled at the company, and rubbed his big stomach over and over, a sign of satisfaction) Following our meeting with the Governor General this morning myself, Sayyid Abdel Azim and Sayyid Omer, we decided to brief you of what had taken place today...then we shall try to explore ways of how we are going to face the present situation. Abdel Azim, would you brief the gentlemen about today's mission? (He then sat properly on his chair and beamed a big smile on everyone in this salon.)

While fiddling with the keys) Abdel Azim thank the Prime Minister and mentioned that based on the resolutions of the Council of Ministers, they decided to see the Governor General and that they had a long discussion with the British, and that they made their point very clear that the British should help us to restore law and order in the South, which Helm at last accepted unconditionally, and that Helm:

> *...tried to be sticky trying to dip his long nose into our affairs, but you know, the Prime Minister lashed on them properly.... Omer here also made his best to show them where they should stand (Stopped briefly to complete his cold lemon juice) But the most important thing is that we managed to make them declare their pledge to support our government (He stopped again to reflect) I should mention that Sir Robertson played a very important role to explain things to his colleagues.*

Omer El Kurdi: Excuse me. I would like to back up what Abdel Azim has said. (Al Azhari permits him feeling certainly satisfied about how things have gone today):

> *...eerr, eerr frankly eerr, eerr Alexander was about to be difficult. Do you know what irritated me; is when he said, "nearly all Southerners I have met felt cheated over Soudanization," and, and then he asked about the "message." I do not know how he knew about it! Anyway, whatever happened, he gave us what we wanted. Gentlemen, I would like*

to tell you frankly (Looking at El Shingaity from the corner of his eyes) that the Prime Minister has proved today that he is truly a wise man a very tactful politician of the first degree. I think few could have done what he did today. He is truly a man of high experience.

Al Azhari: Thank you Omer (Putting on a serious face) In fact what we did today was nothing new but a continuation of our struggle for independence (The big new radio with its big shaking sound at the background is interfering now broadcasting the 8 O'clock evening news. The Prime Minister went on through it to say that:-) When we heard the disturbing news from the South, it was imperative to consult with the Governor General, at least to relief ourselves from any possible responsibility and luckily, we found the man to be of good understanding. Another man in his place could possibly have blown it up costing us the South, or at least, it could have had delayed the celebrations. We had to be tactful. (Al Azhari stopped for a while and said):

> *We met Sir Alexander Knox Helm and Sir James Robertson; by the way Alexander Helm said that when they leave, Chief Justice Aburanat will take over from him to help establish the Sovereign Council of five members.*

Abu Bakr: Aburanat! from which party.
Al Azhari: He told us he is nonpartisan.
Abu Bakr: Nonpartisan; we shall see.
Al Azhari continued his briefing:

> *Sir Alexander then asked me about the message and, and of course, I denied my knowledge of it. They confronted us on the question of Sudanization that Southerners are still unhappy about it and, we defended ourselves very well that there were no qualified Southerners to take over, and that their rights will be preserved and they should not worry (He concludes amid a song over the radio by raising his voice louder) Sir Alexander said, and this is the most important thing; First, he stands by the pledge made in 1947 safeguarding unity of*

the Sudan. Second, he offers the assistance of her Majesty's Government to the new Government of the Sudan to deal with the situation in the South. And also, he condemned the mutiny in the strongest terms possible. Yes, Gentlemen. I think that we have so far achieved our objectives. We want the unity of this country maintained, and the British to carry out their obligations up to the last moments; all these have been achieved.

Abu Bakr preferred to squat on the rug barefooted with his back against the chair. He is now drooling with his sonorous voice and his head to the ground most of the time. He is a well-known old Party member. Tall and skinny, one of his bonny shoulders is exposed and he is toying with his long new turban lying across his laps. He then picked up the point and elaborated:

The Prime Minister has made us accustomed to hearing nothing from him, or about him, but truth. Personally, I am pleased with the results of the talks with the khawajat. But, if I were in the

> *talks, I would have told them to mind their own business on Sudanization (Wagging his long thin index finger) They should know that it was not our fault. How could we assign posts and promote those who are not qualified eh eh how come eh? (Looking around for confirmation and support.)*

Tayifur: (Also looking around for support) They only have themselves to blame and, and those who have been deceiving them, not us…eh …eh?

Omer El Kurdi: Come on, many of these Southerners don't even know how to hold a pen; he said Sudanization, what Sudanization are they talking about? Nonsense.

One of the party members in this salon expressed satisfaction and pledged the support of the Party to the Prime Minister:

> *because the South is a very important part of this country, the Party cannot tolerate anybody who undermines our sovereignty. The Party recommends severe measures on those involved in the mutiny; they should be severely punished. Concerning Aburanat, I know him, he is a good man.*

The other party representative supported the opinions of the last speaker and wondered whether the Opposition would stand by them.

Abu Bakr: Absolutely, the Opposition will stand with us; the South, the South who can give up the South?

Othman Salih El Shingaity: Excuse me, may I say something (Medium height, lighter complexion, and short soft hair. He is just over thirty in age and his is well educated. All kept quiet and turned towards him) From what His Excellency the Prime Minister and the rest of the ministers have said, it becomes clear that there is a problem if not now, in the future.

The guests are immediately aroused with this out-of-step point of view. "Pretentious" El Kurdi remarked silently as he observed this young man expressing his views in a well-balanced Arabic punctuated with some English terminologies such as; you know etc. He continued:

> *"I have come across a report written by the Governor of Bahr el Ghazal yes, Bahr El Ghazal Province (Al Shingaity continued calmly) he says a lot of interesting things in it, very important things (The*

radio is interfering, and nobody could put it off and Omer seems indifferent) One of the things that has drawn my attention in that lengthy report is eerr, eerr when he eerr. eerr he mentioned that, and if I can quote him:

'…that they, "he means Northern Sudanese," can run Omdurman, I believe. That they will soon be fit to govern Rizeigat and the Hadandawa is possible; that they will, in the next two decades be fit to be entrusted with the Zande and the Dinka is even unthinkable.'

Othman took in a deep breath while looking around and up to the ceiling. Then continued:

Your Excellency. I think that we are witnessing the first stage of future events just unfolding ("What events that are unfolding; pretentious," El Kurdi enquired scornfully in silence) I am not pessimistic; I am simply drawing attention to a possible danger. I am therefore advising, if I may, to take care in handling this issue which has now become "the Southern Problem" as a terminology. Usually, big problems start like that, and some politicians would like to use a hammer to crack a nut, and usually this does not work ("Listen, listen to him, go ahead philosopher," mused El Kurdi in silence with some sarcastic smile) instead, results often come out adversely.

El Shingaity continued punctuating his speech with smiles and English here and there for emphasis:

Remember what happened in the Indian subcontinent just a few years ago. A simple problem of Muslim versus Hindu resulted into the fragmentation of that country, and we have now what is called Pakistan. Mr. Prime Minister and gentlemen, I am offering my advice only. Do not rush to crush the South after law and order are established. Always remember to distinguish between citizens and mutineers. This way you isolate the mutineer and choke him and win the citizen to your side otherwise, you will alienate both and possibly lose the whole South ("Real philosopher," El Kurdi remarks silently.)

Al Azhari: I think what Othman has said is very, very important and should be put in mind. Also remember that without his brother, we would probably have no South we are talking about today. Yes, Mohamed Effendi Salih El Shingaity is his brother; he is the man who reached the agreement with the Southerners in 1947 in Juba eh, eh. Othman is speaking to us from knowledge eh, eh. What is going on concerns him very much as it concerns all of us here eh …eh, good.

Omer El Kurdi: Good, Your Excellency. In fact, I want to thank Sayyid, I mean Mr. Othman for his grand ideas sometimes mixed with some philosophy or something like that. I was a bit kind of confused (Some laughter and comments and adds with some big smile) I think this is one of the advantages of getting high education in Europe especially at Oxford (No, Reading University, not Oxford, the Prime Minister corrects with laughter and some humor) El Kurdi continued) But, we should remind ourselves that the South we are talking about with or without people, is a land of strategic importance, isn't it?

El Shingaity: I think I should make myself clearer if I may be allowed:

> *This is a young country, just about to achieve independence. People of the Sudan, as I know, hardly know each other that intimately. It is a country of diverse nationalities, tribes, customs, and traditions ("This is pure philosophy," Omer is remarking silently) An issue like this is always tackled with care aren't they and and, and wisdom isn't? Personally, I stand with the Prime Minister in his position. I also say that South Sudan should be won back gradually using more political instruments rather than pure military ones.*

Abu Bakr: (He is still sitting on the rug and extends one leg for comfort) Omer, our son has totally covered the subject, listen (Pointing at Othman.)

El Kurdi: I am listening, I am getting new ideas.

Party Member: Yes, you better do so, this is education.

Al Azhari: Listen gentlemen. For sure, no one is going to dispute with you Othman on any of the points you have raised. We, as government, are going to correct; Omer-Abdel Azim listen (He laughed with some humor) we are going to correct the situation.

Tayifur: Yes, no matter what it takes.

El Kurdi: Of course, this does not need approval from anybody.

El Shingaity: (He seemed to have got himself involved and cannot retreat, but to continue with these politicians in their game)) May I suggest this (Takes time to reflect and the rest fall silent again while the Prime Minister is watching this young man with a big smile and pride) It is very important for you (Addressing the Prime Minister) to make a public announcement over the Radio, the sooner the better.

Abdel Azim: Why?

El Shingaity: (Still on the stage trying to clarify the point) Yes, you have to explain to the public what has happened in Torit in detail, mention things like who were involved like outside elements if any, the motives of the mutineers, the casualties and… and so on…

Party Member: I think this is a very good idea, truly (Turning to Omer El Kurdi and the rest.)

El Shingaity: (Still on the stage trying to clarify the point) The second thing is that; explain the steps your government has taken so far to restore law and order in the South, and the safeguards. I think all this will cool feelings and will restore confidence in your government.

Tayifur: I absolutely agree with Othman, especially people with relatives in the South are very anxious.

El Shingaity: Sayyid Abdel Azim, the country is under threat…something must be done, isn't it?

El Kurdi: You are right Othman, who cannot see that (Still sitting sideways.)

Al Azhari: Brothers, (Comes in with laughter and some humor) I think the man is correct absolutely. I think I should address the nation after tomorrow, Alexander's address is tomorrow.

Tayifur: That sounds better. We cannot remain silent and let the khawajat speak alone.

Al Azhari: Okay, okay the day after tomorrow, agreed (They all agreed) very well.

The Prime Minister departed to answer a telephone call

at the other end of the salon and in the meantime the guests continued with their conversation. It has been a night of consensus. From hence forth the tempo of the conversation began to slacken.

The hour is getting late as Radio Omdurman late night program of songs had ended and it was now a chance for the Prime Minister to switch the dial to Radio Cairo.

The Prime Minister, who had been moving up and down bare-footed and fiddling with the keys of his new car, came back from the telephone. He was followed silently by Adam, who politely announced to the Prime Minister that dinner is ready. The Prime Minister offered his guests the choice of where they would like to take dinner, in the dining room, or in the court on the grass. Before they reached a decision, Othman Salih El Shingaity got up and with his two hands pulled at the hems of his untagged new snow-white shirt straight down here and there against the blowing wind of the fans. He pulled the shirt again and again while inspecting himself all over, then politely asked for permission from the Prime Minister to leave "because I have another important appointment at this time," checking his new watch.

Tayifur: I am afraid it is another meeting.

El Shingaity: No, of course not. I cannot spend the whole night in meetings.

El Kurdi: Then what? How can one miss a meal like this...?

El Shingaity: In fact, I am invited by those of Ali Al Kheir; it is a promise.

A Party Member: After this nice speech and you want to go, it is a pity.

Al Azhari: (Showing disappointment but with humor) Can't you just wait a little to taste our fish; you have tilapia tonight, Adam, eh?" (Adam answered affirmatively and turned his face away.)

Al Azhari: What is the name of the new cook, the one who has recently come from the Palace of the Governor General eh? ("Musa" Adam supplied the name, Al Azhari turned to the audience) Yes, Musa is the best cook we have so far. He cooked for the Governor General, wallahi.

El Shingaity: (Still standing straight, his hands still pulling at the edge of this new white shirt he had recently brought from London) There is nothing I can do Your Excellency, I am sorry. Those people said they will not taste anything until I come (Giving a look at the watch.)

El Kurdi: Nooooo, no, no, this is a serious problem really, then let him go.

Tayifur: I hope it is not serious like the problem of the South. (All burst into laughter except Adam who is still waiting for instructions where to serve dinner.)

Faced with the dilemma al Azhari helplessly looked at his guests and at Adam trying to figure out what to do. Then again, he invoked the name of Allah and entreated El Shingaity to join them on the table. Once again Othman politely and skillfully turned down the offer expressing regret for having to miss this sumptuous meal, especially Nile tilapia.

After dinner which they had taken in the dining room, Al Azhari called for Adam to clear the tables, and to bring plenty of cold water, lemon juice, ice, the usual drinks and especially the Governor General's gift which he had brought along with him from Scotland. During this course, Omer El Kurdi turned down the hot drinks and confined himself to beer only.

Party Member: What is wrong with you Omer, eh?

El Kurdi: in fact, I have never consumed alcohol even

when I was a small boy in the village. When I was on a tour in England, and it was so cold, some friends invited me, you know. I thought it was a chance to learn. Oh, I spent the whole night vomiting; from that moment I never tasted it.

Abu Bakr: Poor man, you are missing life.

After a short while, Abu Bakr raised his arm up in the air snapping his fingers over and over, an expression of total admiration of a song flowing from the gramophone at the far end of the salon. Then abruptly he calmed down and said with apparent heavily loaded head, "I…I…bet those of Othman are now dancing" (He meandered and snapped his fingers in the air while seated on the rug) "Those boys are tough; they are tough; I know."

Voices are subdued, and it is very late. At last, the Prime Minister walked his guests to their respective cars and bade them farewell, and they too wished him well. After that he wobbled back into his bedroom. It had been a very long and busy day.

CHAPTER FOUR

Too Late

Sir Alexander and Lady Knox Helm, Sir James Robertson, Mr. and Mrs. J Jones and Mr. Nigel Crawford gathered on the lawn of the Governor General's residence within the compound of the Palace. Also, present were Christine and Mary Ann, daughters of the Governor General. Although it was a social occasion, conversation centered on this morning's meeting with the Prime Minister and the situation in the Sudan in general.

After dinner, the Helms and their guests retired to more comfortable armchairs while the servants, including Katta, studiously cleared the tables. More drinks were brought and carefully placed on their respective tables, while two of the caterers started to serve. The guests and the hosts chatted in calm voices sometimes punctuated by subdued laughter, especially from the ladies and the two little girls. These are their last weeks in the Sudan and this gathering reminds them of home.

Sir Alexander: Ladies and gentlemen, Mr. Ismael Al Azhari and two of his ministers saw me this morning. Sir Robertson was present. As the situation demanded, I authorized him to take necessary measures to handle conditions in the South and assured him of the help of Her Majesty's Government. I should say that after hearing the disturbing news, I received instructions from the British Prime Minister to help restore law and order. There's fear the ramifications of a breakaway South Sudan on the East African possessions could be negative. Incidentally, I heard these people use the same argument. Yes, moreover it was thought that Britain's non-interference may force the Sudanese to call for Egyptian military gamble and this might undermine our leading role in this part of the world, you know.

Besides, (The Governor General continued) the French

and the Belgians are across the border; I mean it is quite a dilemma you know. Anyway, instructions were very clear; appeal to the rebels to surrender with guarantees for fair trials and persuade the Arabs to adopt a more conciliatory approach to the issue. You know that each nation has a set of values tempered by their basic beliefs and so on; the Arabs have their beliefs. But, in as much as the Arabs seem to lack sense of justice and truthfulness, some people believe so; these values are among the greatest characteristics of the Anglo-Saxons instilled by Judaic-Christian values, long experience and history. During the last five score years or so; I wonder whether we have been fair to the people of this country.

Sir Alexander reached for the glass of beer, checked the time, and took out his pipe to smoke.

Lady Helm: Alexander and I have debated the issue and hardly disagreed (She is just over fifty, medium in height though not so strikingly beautiful now, and though she is fairly educated, she has learned how to express herself in the best possible way. To night she is in her fine evening bright-blue dress. She continued) He is a faithful servant of the Crown but seems not to see the rationale behind the decision uniting these seemingly rather unrelated peoples, poor Alexander.

Mr. Nigel Crawford: (Chief of the Intelligence, is short and not so heavily built, he had two sharp blue eyes and short whiskers framing his little tough face) As far as I guess Lady Helm, there is no rationale. You see, before Gordon, these people have been together on the Nile, and time has come to leave, you know. I think our job is to try to make them come back to each other again; it may take some time. May I remind that I met this MP Dominic; Domenico Mourwel; he was a priest. I invited him to stand with me and see what was to become of the first Council of Ministers in session, he stubbornly refused. Anyway, let us hope that one day they will learn to live together and create a nation. (He then added with an eye on Sir Robertson) Sure, the blacks will require more time to catch up and eventually they will if given enough guarantees, I should hope.

Sir James Robertson: (Heavily built, medium height with dark sunburnt rough skin that explains the number of years he had spent in the Sudan. His grey thinning hair is smoothly pressed back) Domenico is a typical Southerner if I may say, sort of a revolutionary; but as a matter of fact, I have often met some of the Southerners, who sport ideas like those he has. In all, we still have a delicate situation here. Prior to the Conference in 1947, we had three unpleasant options, Lady Helm. Some thought the South was purely African and should be annexed to one of the East African possessions, you see. Others thought it should be developed on separate lines leading to independence; there was fear of the French and the Belgians. But after lengthy discussions here and at home, consensus was on unification of the Sudan, you see. But now, I and others are aware of the anomaly. However, the decision was based on certain overriding considerations, or so it was thought.

J Jones: (Intervened) May you explain, Sir.

Sir Robertson: Very well; for example, Egyptian interests didn't favor any creation of another state along the Nile. Moreover, besides racial, and cultural differences, it was thought that history, geography and economics have welded these people sufficiently to become inextricably bound. I think the problem is simple, Mr. Jones, Mr. Crawford; they may stay together for a while and, later, resort to some sort of a constitutional arrangement to settle their differences.

J Jones: (A slim figure. Tonight, he is in a full grey light suit without a necktie. He is in mid-thirties and therefore young and full of energy and ideals) When I was in the Foreign Office, I heard and read much about Sudan; the Mahdi, Gordon and I thought it was a fabulous country only to be struck in the face.

Sir Robertson: Easy, Mr. Jones easy. It always starts like that but after some time you fall in love, only that these are the last days.

J Jones: (Giving a big smile) I mean, these people don't even share a bit of anything to back up the argument (He directed this point to Robertson and Mr. Nigel and turned to his wife just next to him, and continued) Personally, I have misgivings regarding the viability of this country, I mean how can Sudan be far from India and Pakistan?

Lady Helm: Exactly. Gentlemen, we've already seen it happening and this is before independence. We saw India split; good God it was awful. Let's pray Sudan doesn't follow.

Sir Robertson: Don't worry Mrs. Helm. This country was united under certain provisions and now they've started to have problems, we expect the Arabs to have learned and begin to look at Southerners with respect.

Mr. Crawford: I beg your pardon Sir. Mr. Owens' recommendations expressed strong misgivings and seemed to suggest some sort of autonomy if they have to be united at all.

Sir Robertson: Thank you. You've reminded me of the 40s, arguments and counterarguments. Ladies and gentlemen, you see autonomies don't work in poor societies where political awareness is very low, especially in the South. At any rate that's too late now.

Sir Alexander Helm had been listening while smoking his pipe quietly. What could he do? It is now too late as Sir James Robertson has just uttered. In a matter of the coming few weeks, the Union Jack will be folded and a new chapter in the history of the Sudan will unfold. He felt some cool breeze blowing from the South; "Rain must have fallen down there," he guessed. Quietly in his chair, he had already visualized Nigeria; an ethnic mosaic with heavy religious overtones; Muslims in the north, Christians in the South and wondered who created such countries, "The devil who creates such countries; there must be many Robertsons out there; look at India, China, Nigeria and God knows where else; Rhodesia and South Africa, and here in Sudan; all are race and religion infested," he murmured silently. Kitchener's apparition flickered and he tried to clear it but in vain. Finally, Sir Alexander yelled at Kitchener's apparition; "Why, why did you do it Herbert, why? The French fellow was correct. Didn't you hear him yonder there down the Nile; in Fashoda? Was Khalifa's blood not enough to quench your thirst, didn't Charles's soul finally rest in peace? Now see what you've done; this country, these ruins, your jackals are howling and snarling and already would tear themselves apart; nonsense, nonsense." Sir Robertson's 'too late' jolted him back into the discussion circle. As the BBC wound up the international news, Sir Alexander Knox Helm returned into this small British circle. He lowered the volume of the radio and sat upright.

Sir Helm: Ladies and gentlemen, today I have given my word to stand by the Prime Minster in his efforts to end…. this mutiny or is it disturbance. I am doing this as a servant of Her Majesty, at other times I could not have done so (He stopped for a while, then continued and all the eyes are fixed on him except those of Mary Ann who was busy with her own affairs there on the late evening loan of the Palace) My conviction is that, South and North are not related, and I wish there was a better way to save the situation for both and, spare them the pain. I pray to the Lord that all will be well for the people of the Sudan.

This time he asked the servant to serve him with a glassful of whisky. He sipped it and then put it on the table and leaned his head against the chair to watch Mary Ann playing thereon the grass, with the moon behind her rising like a large silver ball.

By now the sky had cleared, the dust had settled. Mrs. Helm leaned on her husband's shoulder and felt his head with her hand and held his hand in sympathy and support. She had already felt they were on their way home; those high lovely Scottish mountains and the Scottish country life. The rest continued to exchange views, though calmly.

Mr. Nigel Crawford picked up a new subject arguing that Islam was irrelevant to the people of the South, while Sir Robertson thought the opposite may be correct.

Sir Robertson: Look, just look at them, Mr. Crawford, look at their manners. I mean their habits and customs; you know, aren't much different from those of the Mohammadans. I tend to agree with Duncan, as a matter of fact, Islam could be more suitable to them considering their ways of life.

Mr. Crawford: how? I don't understand, sir.

J Jones: (Facing Sir Robertson) What makes you think so, sir?

Sir Robertson: People there marry and divorce just like that (Snapping his fingers, then continued but more seriously) I mean this is what Mohammadans do, isn't it, and exactly this is what these people need, don't you think so, sir?

J Jones: Well, I don't know much about that, but I thought we had a moral obligation towards them, at least.

Sir Robertson: Well, I think that is too late now, I'm afraid Mr. Jones.

J Jones: Okay, then what are the guarantees they will not be subjected to some sort of a fanatical warfare in the future?

Sir Robertson: Islam will not be imposed on anybody even in South Sudan, you know.

Mr. Crawford: I beg to disagree with you Sir. I'm afraid that Islam will be imposed, judging from history.

J Jones: Then I'm afraid Southerners won't be able to

participate in the system in an Arab-dominated country.

Sir Robertson: There is a draft constitution that will solve this problem; it proposes that, "There shall be no discrimination on the basis of religion, race or color…" in appointments to constitutional and any other civil service posts you see.

Mr. Crawford: Long after we've gone and the Southerners left to their fate, anything can happen, I'm afraid sir (Sounding cynical.)

At this point, Lady Helm decided to intervene by expressing that, while nothing could be done now, she felt that Southerners were not fairly treated in 1947 because their representatives were not given enough opportunity to weigh things and appraise consequences of the deal they were about to enter. On his part, Sir Robertson tried to explain to her the steps he took to bring the issue to the notice of the Southerners and that his conviction was that the representatives of the South at that time were capable to express themselves sufficiently.

Mrs. Clara Jones, a tall elegant young woman with short hair hanging just above her shoulders and two long blue earrings matching her evening dress, somewhat timidly came into the conversation trying to make a point, after all Mrs. Helm had been participating in the discussion.

Mrs. Jones: Sir Robertson, may I ask?

Sir Robertson: Yes, my dear Clara (All eyes are fixed on her.)

Mrs. Jones: May I ask you, sir,

Sir Robertson: Yes, go ahead (Attention is focused on Clara.)

Mrs. Jones: (Adjusts herself to sit more properly pulling her dress more tightly down her knees) In 1947 if I recall, you allowed a group of Chiefs to meet with highly educated people, knowledgeable of the law and the art of government in just two days, and…

Sir Robertson: Yes, go ahead.

Mrs. Jones: Did you expect a favorable result for the Southerners?

Sir Robertson: This is a good question. First, allow me to make this point clear, dear Madam (His face turned sort of rigid) The decision to unite the Sudan was not originally mine; I was merely carrying out my duties as servant of the Crown. Now whether the representation of the South was adequate or not, is subjective in my opinion, you know.

(Lowered his voice a little but directed his speech to Mrs. Jones):

> *You see, in those days it was impossible to find a Southerner with sufficient education, those few were Missionary educated, just enough to read the Bible and perhaps to do some clerical work. You can't imagine how backward these people were. So, we thought of the Chiefs because as tribal communities Chiefs may bargain a little harder. And when we found out on the second day that the two parties had agreed on the terms of their unity, we were there only to attest to what they had agreed upon.*

Mrs. Jones: (Smiling) I don't want to be thought of being sympathetic. I'm just curious. Sir, in your opinion, don't you think these people have been conned by the Arabs?

Mr. Crawford: That is a very good question.

Sir Robertson: Yeeaah, that is a good question (Looking at Crawford and Mr. and Mrs. Helm) but, know Mrs. Jones, again you have reminded me of those days; No, there are provisions in the agreement that guarantee some of the basic rights of the people in the South of the Sudan to education, to economic and social development and to a fair political representation you know. (At this point Mr. Crawford interjects.)

Mr. Crawford: Then what was the best justification to unite these peoples?

Sir Robertson: (Beginning to feel uncomfortable; these are his last days, and he is demanded to make himself clearer) Oh dear; you see (Avoiding Mr. Crawford) Mrs. Jones, all arrangements were made with the best interests of the South in mind. However, you yourself may have seen them around. They don't have leaders to speak to, you know; I mean they don't have this sense of (Looking for the right expression) togetherness you know, and and nationhood you know, at least up to this moment.

Mr. J Jones: (Could not wait any long) So, it was thought better to keep them with the Arabs for a while till they develop those senses, sir?

Mr. Crawford: I think that was the idea.

Sir Robertson: You see, in the future, they may rise up as a strong people, and the Arabs will have to reckon with that. I think only if they embrace Islam should this country be truly stable. And if they don't, that will be the end of it.

Mr. Jones: What a price!

Mrs. Helm: (Groaning) Poor Africans.

Christine: (She is about twelve years old. She has her hair tied up with a red ribbon and thrown on her back. She and her sister study in London) Sir Robertson (She is asking in a squeaky voice) how did Southerners become Christians, was it imposed, I see them in church.

Sir Robertson: That is a nice piece of a question indeed dear Christie. You see, eer when we first arrived, Africa was largely animist and heathen, you understand; I mean, they didn't have spiritually organized religions you know…like Christianity. They worshiped spirits of their ancestors and the like; you know. Then we encouraged priests to come and do some vocation you know, preaching the Gospel and, and at the same time help us tame them.

Christine: (Her eyes enlarged with horror) Are they still savages; do they eat people?

Sir Robertson: Noooo, that is not true, (Smiling at her) that is not true at all my dear, they don't eat people, understand.

The hour is getting late. The moon is approaching

the middle of the sky; Sir Alexander Knox Helm made a motion to wind up the evening.

Sir Alexander Helm: Ladies and gentlemen, Mrs. Helm, the two little girls and I, shall leave within the coming few weeks (He casts his eyes down to collect idea) I think Chief Justice Mohamed Ahmed Aburanat will be able to run affairs in an efficient manner as a caretaker Governor General; he has some experience; the rest shall be their affairs. Sir Robertson, you will depart for Nigeria as soon as the Union Jack is lowered. The coming few weeks will be trying (He takes in a fresh breath to wind up) This young government has cried out for help. As agreed, you will contact the Foreign Office and I will be in touch with East Africa. Let's pray this is the last mutiny we're ever involved in. Ladies and gentlemen, it has been a night, a useful one.

Sir Robertson: Thank you, Sir. I shall miss your kind guidance. Doubtless history will record the decisive role you've played in helping the Sudanese achieve their long-cherished goal. I believe that the dramatic events that had taken place are now behind us. Let's do what we can and leave the rest to history. (Turned to Mrs. Helm) I beg your pardon Mrs. Helm; you've been such a noble woman.

I hope that we shall meet again at happier times (Then turned to Christine and held Mary Ann's little hand who was fighting sleep) school will soon open and you should catch up eh. Your mother and father are such nice people, please be nice to them eh, okay, good girls and good night (Turned to Mrs. and Mr. J Jones giving a long smile a long smile) We shall meet in England hopefully after Nigeria.

The moon had reached the middle of the sky, and all rose to leave wishing each other the sweetest of dreams. Sir Alexander and Mrs. Helm walked their guests to the gate, leaving sleepy Mary Ann lying on one of the chairs.

CHAPTER FIVE

Farewell, Governor

This morning Monday December 19, 1955, Parliament is full. All the Senators, the Deputies, the Ministers, the dignitaries, and the guests have taken their seats. In addition, a few senior British and Egyptian colonial officials have also occupied a section of the House and sitting next to them is Janet, the only female in this big hall. One of the front rows to the left of the podium is reserved for the notables and religious leaders, both Muslim and Coptic Christians.

Sitting among the religious leaders is Father Boulus Iskandar. He is representing the Coptic and the entire

Christian community in the Sudan. He is in long, all-black priestly vestment. His eyes are wide open rolling around, scanning this decorated august hall while stoking his long white beard and checking this large black crucifix dangling down his large chest. He is now about seventy-six years old since he escaped death in the massacre in the compound of the Palace of the Governor General some seventy years ago. Since that time, he seems not to have forgotten some details of that horrific massacre that Al Mahdi forces carried out early in the morning of 26 January 1885.

To the left of Father Boulus Iskandar are Abdelrahman Al Mahdi, now about seventy-three years old, Alsadiq Al Siddiq Abdelrahman Al Mahdi is seventeen years old, a student at Daniel Comboni Secondary School. He is already entertaining a vision that the British and the Egyptians will soon be history; look at his long thin face and mouth murmuring, "This is our country and soon we shall be the masters," the young man was looking far into the future.

Abdelrahman Al Mahdi is black, which he seems to have inherited from his mother, since Al Mahdi was known to have had numerous wives and unknown number of concubines from different ethnic and tribal backgrounds in Sudan.

Although his back was bending, Sheikh Abdelrahman seemed healthy. His eyes met with those of Father or Abuna Boulus and the two reached for each other for a greeting. Nigel, who was sitting behind them, felt obliged to get up to greet the two religious men and this young man called Al Sadiq and those close by. Sheikh Abdelrahman continued to count these long beads in what seemed like silent prayers. Other members of Al Mahdi family were lined up followed by Ali Al Mirghani and some members of his family.

Buried in his chair, Sheikh Abdelrahman suddenly recalled when he visited London and how he offered the sword of his father to the King; "King George was very happy when I offered him the sward of my father; Buckingham Palace is very large, very large within a very large garden. I was very much impressed with all I had seen." Sheikh Abdelrahman Al Mahdi recalled; "The English are polite, very respectful people; see how they received us, like we were kings." Preparations were going on, "King George was about to install me king over the Sudan ... I could have been king if I had accepted the offer; see that small girl, Eliazabath, she is now the Queen."

Amid preparations, Sheik Abdelrahman had a brief spell of a vision; how he and two of his half-brothers, Bushra, and Al Siddiq narrowly escaped death at the hands of General Reginald Wingate that cold morning in Umdubeikerat on 22 November 1898; "Hey boys, keep your eyes open, the English are not far from here," the Ansari sternly warned us. "We fearfully kept awake till midnight anticipating an attack at any moment, and then I drifted and suddenly I got jolted by a very loud terrifying sound of a bomb and the Ansari got hold of my hand and we began to run in panic; machine guns were spraying bullets all over the place. He pulled me this way and that way to evade the soldiers until we were out of firing range. I was shivering all over, but Allah saved us, "Thank Allah, thank Allah," The Ansari kept pulling my hand and urged us to run till we were far."

In the meantime, preparations were feverishly underway as loudspeakers were being noisily tested. Sheikh Abdelrahman continued in his daydreaming, "The sun was up, we crossed the river, and then we were told that we had reached Al Shukaba village and that we were safe from the English. Why did Wingate want to kill us, why?" He was murmuring. "Thank Allah, thank Allah, here I'm witnessing the last departure of the English. Anyway, this country is ours and we are its masters."

Preparations were going and the entourage of the Prime Minister and the outgoing Governor General was expected at any moment.

The gallery was tightly packed with various party leaders, notables, supporters, and leaders of different religious sects. Banners carrying slogans such as "Aliens go home," and "Sudan is for the Sudanese" and others lauding the Prime Minister for his valiant role in the struggle for independence, and those carrying "Long live free and independent Sudan" were sprawling outside the Hall. The Communists and other left-leaning activists have their all-red banners screaming slogans, such as "Imperialists go home." It is a free country.

The arrangement placed members of the Black Bloc MPs in a row just opposite that of minister David Angundit, minister Baluong and minister Alfred Wani. Not far from Father Dominic, was Father Philip Abbas Ghabush of the Anglican Church from the Nuba Mountains and this tall thin MP called Ibrahim Deriej from Darfur Province who later became Governor of Darfur State. Before becoming a priest, Philip Abbas Ghabush was a local wrestler who had never been thrown down at all. He had a square face, large square shoulders, a large square chest, had large square palms and thick legs. He was hot tempered. The man was hell of a wrestler; but fate, or may it be the Holy Spirit, made him to be a priest and a politician. All along, the priest, in a black suit and no necktie, sat with focused open chest and open red eyes. There is going to be a wrestling today; no, it is a hot debate.

Squeezed in this throng on the balcony was this seven years old Lazarus Dhieu, who had arrived from the South a week or two before the mutiny in 1955. In this tiny space his attention seemed divided, for he kept an eye on his uncle Deputy Domenico Muorwel who, in a dark suit, was sitting rigidly in the middle of the Southern Sudanese Members of Parliament. At the same time, this small boy was trying to follow up the frantic slogan chanters on the balcony around him. Right now, there is buzzing and shouting in the hall, and there were shouting voices outside the Parliament building.

At twenty minutes past nine in the morning, the motorcade entered the gate of the Parliament compound amid a storm of hand clapping and slogan chanting clearly heard by Lazarus and the rest of those inside the building. Three men stepped out of their respective cars and together walked to the podium to receive a salute from the guards of honor. After inspecting the guards, they entered the hall to be received with another storm of applause and some disconcerted chanting from the balcony.

Now it was becoming clear to Lazarus what was this all about. Standing on tiptoes most of the time, and extending his long thin neck, he could see this round figure in white suit and this white man (He is a Turuk as Lazarus knows natives call white people) The three men acknowledged this rapturous reception as the three men kept smiling and waving most of the time. After a while, the three men sat on their white cloth covered chairs, and down everybody sat and suddenly there was a hush in the hall.

Abdalla Surur, a World War II veteran military officer turned into a politician, was presiding over the joint session of the House of Representatives and the Senate. Everybody was in place as the radio announcer declared live from his position in the corner of the hall. Speaker Abdalla Surur then picked up the gavel, banged on the table to call the Joint House to session.

After the Koran recitation, a succession of political leaders and poets delivered fire-igniting speeches or so it seemed to Lazarus from the balcony. However, it seemed that all this was just a prelude to the main event still to come. In their speeches, the speakers seemed to lambast the mutineers, some of them called for the government to hit them with an iron fist "so that they should not entertain that heinous idea again," as Deputy Sinada put it. Watching all this hullaballoo, Lazarus could not comprehend what was exactly taking place.

Amid all this commotion the Speaker called upon Deputy Abdel Rahman Dabka from Kurdufan Province. Deputy Dabka approached the microphone in a self-assured manner as he kept checking his jellabiya, touching and adjusting his turban here and there. Lazarus extended his neck to observe. Dabka blew through the microphone once, twice while looking around with red eyes. Again, he blew through the microphone and knocked at it so that it was loudly heard outside the Hall. He stopped for a while to search his two pockets. He got out a piece of paper and began to read after reminding the House that he had a short statement to read. Then Dabka reached this paragraph at which he began to be sort of fidgety, nevertheless, he read through; "Therefore, Mr. Speaker therefore, allow me to declare here now that we, we, we the members of this House, of this august House unanimously, declare in the name of all the people of the Sudan that now Sudan has become a completely free and independent country (A deafening applause) We therefore, call upon His Excellency the Prime Minister to ask the two governments of the Condominium; England and Egypt, to declare their recognition immediately," again the Joint House exploded into a prolonged applause and slogan chanting.

The Joint House fell silent when the Speaker pointed at someone at the far right who hurriedly reached for the microphone. Apparently shaking with emotions, this man seemed agitated because his hands were trembling as he reached for the microphone. He too blew into the microphone three times, "I second the motion because Sudan is no longer a colony, but a free sovereign country just like Great Britain, and Egypt also."

Amid this wind of applause, Lazarus began to see some sense especially with all the chanting, the strong fist clenching and air jabbing. Suddenly somebody startled him with a wild shriek who went on shouting over and over "independence, freedom, liberty," and suddenly Lazarus remembered his uncle briefed him in the morning that they were going to bid farewell to the Turuk Governor General and after that Sudan will be free; free from what, or from whom, this was what he could not understand. Rather, he wondered why all this chanting and fist clenching and air jabbing. But all the same, it was an event worth watching.

Speaker Abdalla Surur called upon Deputy Abdel Khaliq Mahjoub whose identity was rumored on the balcony as the Secretary General of the Communist Party of the Sudan. He had a round head, round face, round shoulders, thick round chest, he was in his thirties and was somewhat flamboyant. He sprang up immediately and hurriedly approached the microphone. He waited for the shouting to calm down, then started his speech by thanking the Speaker. Without roundabouts and courtesy, Abdel Khaliq Mahjoub delved into history, recounting how Sudan unjustly fell victim to Anglo-Egyptian imperialism, how Sudan was exploited economically and rendered poor and powerless, especially how the British treacherously planted seeds of sedition "between us and our brothers in the South which exploded into a violent conflict on the eve of our independence and that by the might of "our armed forces and assistance from the democratic, progressive and peace-loving countries, we shall crush this mutiny and this shall be a lesson to all imperialists and their lackeys to learn." He went on to call upon the "imperialists and their lackeys to depart right now, not tomorrow," and that they should know that "Sudan is for the Sudanese;" he is reminded to wind up, "yes, yes I know just a minute," big smiles and red eyes are shooting out. Abdel Khaliq Mahjoub ended by shouting "long live free united Sudan long, live the forces of democracy and Socialism, long live the struggle of the masses, long live the unity of the working forces and death to international imperialism." There was intense applause from the end of the Hall and some slogan chanting from a section of the Hall.

Lazarus observed silence and grim faces from certain sections of the House and especially from the Black Bloc.

One of the highlights of this extraordinary session that attracted Lazarus's attention was the long poem delivered by Ali Al Ja'ali, excerpts read as follows:

At last, at long last,
With a radiant face thou have emerged,
With the banner of liberty firmly in thy hand,
Confidently Al Azhari, forward march,
Forward neither turn, nor look back not,
Closely behind thee we firmly stand,
To strengthen thee, and they back protect,
From all those who, may thee wish harm.

Apparently inspired by the recent events in the South, Al Ja'ali continued using all the oratory skills he could master and those he could conjure or instantly invent. His thin frame would shake, and he had to fight to keep this worn-out turban from falling off his small head. Lazarus took time to watch this reed-like figure profoundly as he threw this small, clenched fist up, jabbed the air or so it seemed. And then Al Ja'ali would point that sharp stiff thin finger far away, then downright in front of him. Ali Al Ja'ali continued breathing fire from his long reedy neck in the following verses:

> *The South, Al Azhari, the South is truly precious,*
> *On it, compromise not,*
> *Neither with the imperialists nor with their lackeys,*
> *I say with those miserable souls consult not,*
> *Miserable souls to imperialists are always cronies,*
> *With an iron fist, Al Azhari, with an iron fist,*
> *Hit them, and their little homes destroy,*
> *Under thy feet crush them, their fire stem out,*
> *So that proudly the coming generations,*
> *Shall inherit a land of peace and dignity.*

Though they may have not understood anything, the Deputies and Senators from South Sudan, some nineteen or so as Lazarus could guess, lumped up together sat through with faces of stone. Lazarus knew later that some of the Deputies and Senators did take part in the Juba Conference in 1947.

Speaker Abdalla Surur, who seemed to have been highly tantalized by Ali Al Ja'ali, had to take some time to recompose before he could bring the House back to order.

Another speaker was called upon. This notable personality spoke at length about the significance of independence in the wake of the defeat of the mutineers, "especially at this junction of the history of the Arab nation." He ended by stressing the importance of holding on to the South, "because, the South is the natural extension of the Arab nation into Africa heartland."

To the surprise of Lazarus, his uncle, Deputy Dominic Muorwel, was called upon. The Honorable Deputy approached the microphone while adjusting his green-striped necktie. He was to speak in English. He started by thanking the Speaker "for this great chance you have given me," and proceeded in a calm voice though somewhat strained but apparently struggling to make his English as standard as possible; "Mr. Speaker Sir, he continued:

> *When the Turks first came here into this land of ours…they found different tribes and races forming this county called Sudan living together, but the Southerners in the South and the Northerners here in the North (He took deep breath then continued) And when the British came to colonize the Sudan together with the Egyptians in a Condominium, they too found us living together in this land of*

ours, but the Northerners in the North and the Southerners in the South but look. Today, as we approach independence, we are seeing new developments taking shape (Rounding his hands in the air to demonstrate what he means, then he raises his voice in a clear emotion as he continues) Mr. Speaker, Mr. Speaker, why why is the government sending Northerners to the South in great numbers, why? (He cools down as he drags on) eerr. eerr another point to dwell upon Mr. Speaker, is the point of eer, eer constitutional set up of…this country. We eerr, eerr the representatives from the South would like the Prime Minister to clearly promise now, in this session, to implement federalism. Federalism is our only demand as it was agreed upon in 1947, and it should be implemented before the British administrators could finally depart.

Then he turned back to his seat and Lazarus heard some applause from the MPs of the South. The Joint House was still buzzing and there was more to come, it seemed.

Father Saturnino O'hure Hilange was sitting quietly

among his MP colleagues; his eyes are large and bright as ever. He was in all white priestly robes. Like most of the MPs from South Sudan that morning, he was young, and in as much as he was a politician, he happened to know the limits of his spiritual profession that dictates moral respect; also, he was a politician who knew how to tackle practical issues up to the required limits, "Politics is a dirty game," he was reminded. But above all, Father Saturnino O'hure Hilange was a revolutionary in spirit and no one should make a mistake about that. To prove that he gave a blind eye to the church and contested and won elections while in full priestly uniform.

But destiny and chance sometimes dictate their terms as was in this crucial moment in history, and this was manifested in this session of the Joint House of Parliament. In this historic session, ironically, Father Saturnino was conscious that he was representing two constituencies, the people of South Sudan with their aspirations, and the Church with her obligations. Today is the day, either to be or not to be. He knew he was here not only to speak, but to fight, express and to articulate the hopes and aspirations of his constituencies, the people of South Sudan, and the mother church. After two or three speakers, Father Saturnino was called upon.

In a long white priestly vestment, this tall priest with large white eyes, upward shooting hair, got up and walked to the microphone. He was confident but a little bit shaken; no, he was tense. Why should he not be tense; in fact, the whole House was tense for every single Member of Parliament, Senate, and Ministers in the new government, every notable and all the members of the departing British and Egyptian colonial officials, everyone was tense for this was an occasion that may not come around again. But will there be ears that will listen to some of the angry or prophetic words that will be uttered today.

The Father grabbed the microphone, blew through it and began to pound on the basic issues for which he was here. Using revolutionary tone and the best English vocabulary he could master, the Father touched on so many subjects and on so many aspects of the problem of the South, expressing fear on independence. Then he lowered his voice to read this concluding statement:

> *Mr. Speaker Sir. The South has no ill-intentions whatsoever toward the north; the South simply claims the right to run its local affairs in a united Sudan. The South has no intention of separating from the North, for has that been the case, nothing on earth would have prevented the demand for separation. The South is demanding to federate with the North, the right that the South undoubtedly possesses as a consequence of the principle of free self-determination, which reason and democracy grant to a free people. The South will, at any moment separate from the North if and when the North so desires through socio-economic and political subjugation of the South.*

There was some applause from the Deputies from the South, but the Hall remained buzzing. The ceiling is high, and the newly fitted fans were swirling at a high speed. The Radio announcer and the translator who were sitting in their corner seemed confused, not knowing how to translate the Father's message live. Meanwhile, the crowd outside was unaware of what was going on in the Hall.

After several speakers were called and spoke, Wilson Andrago was called upon. A fire-eating revolutionary, he too began to pound on so many issues:

> *If this is independence, we don't want it, yes, we don't want it. That is why, that is why some of us in Juba Conference tried tototo, toto to, to refuse unity so that we should not be mistreated like we are already seeing. Now our offices down there in the South are already full, full to the brim with Northerners, some of them even do not know how to read and write English (He was interrupted repeatedly for point of order and was reminded to watch his language, nevertheless, Andrago dragged on) Mr. Speaker Sir, Mr. Speaker Sir I for one strongly object to this policy of Arabization andandand and and Islamization that has just come up, because, in doing so Mr. Speaker Sir, you, you are going tototo to, to lose, to lose the South forever yes, forever.*

Deputy Wilson Andrago swept his arm across the Hall in an angry mood, and he was reminded to watch his language and time.

> *Mr. Speaker Sir, as my colleague pointed out here before, I call upon this Parliament House to decide now and not tomorrow to give the South federalism. Federalism is our only demand and if not put into action, there will be problems in this country of ours lying in store.*

The Speaker banged on the table to remind Andrago to be brief.

> *Okay, okay to finish Mr. Speaker Sir, to conclude I think the best way to put an end to this so-called Southern Problem federalism is, is the only solution, thank you Mr. Speaker Sir.*

As soon as Andrago finished his speech, the Deputies from the South, few as they are, clapped their hands noisily and more enthusiastically than otherwise expected; was this an attempt to impress the House, or was it an act of defiance tacitly enquired Mr. Nigel Crawford who had been sitting stiff neck; look at Ms. Janet, this small size Irish woman, she was smiling, why? While some of the Northern Deputies looked grim and depressed because of Andrago's speech and earlier similar speeches, others were apparently exasperated and would throw angry looks towards their Southern colleagues. Passions from both sides soared high but wait.

Sayyid Mohamed Ahmed Mahjoub, a highly intellectual and seasoned lawyer of the time and one of the prominent leaders of the opposition who later became Prime Minister; shrewd and intelligent, he was acknowledged so by many in Sudan, an arrogant self-conceited man by any conceivable degree as strongly believed by many South Sudanese, was called upon.

He took time to rise for he seemed not to be in a hurry. At the microphone, he surveyed the Joint House with those large red eyes which have become larger on this occasion. He reached for his papers and then cleared his sonorous voice to speak. He welcomed the outgoing Governor General, the Prime Minister and all the guests attending this historic occasion held to consider, among the issues, the question of self-determination now turned into independence. He thanked Deputy Dabka for the motion and urged the Joint House to bless it, and pointed at this historic day as "the day for which we have been fighting for, our fathers and our forefathers had died for, a dream come true…"

In contrast, Deputy Mohamed Ahmed Mahjoub referred to the mutiny as a "minor security issue which had taken place a few months ago in Torit." However, he accused the government of Prime Minister Al Azhari for being too slow, and too soft on the issue, and called for draconian measures to nip this mutiny in the bud "because this is the only way to deal with the mutineers," and "this is one of many ways to preserve the unity of the country," and urged the Minister of Defense to act more swiftly and firmly by "sending more troops to the South to maintain law and order." He reminded some of the members of the House not to be carried away by their passions but to "put the interests of the Sudan above any other consideration as a new page in the history of this country is just being opened." He went on to lash those "half-hearted Deputies whose loyalty to the nation is on the balance…"

All along this speech, Lazarus Dhieu could notice how quiet the House was, then would erupt into a sustained applause except the Deputies from the South of Sudan, but Minister David Angundit among the Southerners was showing those big white teeth; was he happy with what was going on, was he admiring the speakers, or was he merely smiling, and why; Lazarus could not understand.

As soon as Sayyid Mohamed Ahmed Mahjoub finished his speech the Joint House erupted into intense applause and some slogan chanting, and with-it tension rose higher between the Black Bloc MPs and some of the nearby northern Deputies. Murmurs of disapproval and clenched fist showing, angry eyeballs and some insults were traded across this section of the Hall. Suddenly, Lazarus saw Deputy Lual and Deputy Stanislaus struggling to pull back Deputy Dominic who was within an inch from the neck of the nearest Northern Sudanese Deputy. To control the row, Sayyid Abdalla Surur had to keep banging on the table and shouted asking for calm and order.

When order was finally restored, the Speaker took time to comment making whatever possible to water down what Deputy Saturnino and Deputy Wilson had said earlier alluding to that as a possible cause of ill-feelings among the countrymen; he concluded in his husky voice, "Such talk at this delicate moment is serious:

> *and definitely does not serve the cause of unity in our country. After all, we are brothers, and and any, any problem no matter how difficult or thorny, can be discussed calmly and and a solution found.*

The Speaker introduced the Prime Minister. On the podium Ismail Al Azhari adjusted his dark blue spotted tie and cleared his throat several times to prepare to speak. Suddenly he gave a big smile to the Hall while rocking his large trunk and raised his thick hands to wave to the audience on the balcony in response to their slogan chanting. Lazarus could see the Radio announcer busy introducing the Prime Minister to the eager nation.

Although it was winter and it was cold out there, yet fans were swirling at full speed under the high ceiling of the House of Parliament. After checking his papers, the voice of the Prime Minister sneaked through into the microphone and into the air as it was being broadcast live: Al

Azhari cleared his throat to speak. Mr. Governor General Sir Alexander Knox Helm, our dear great friend, Sir James Robertson, our departing Egyptian brothers (Intense applause and some slogan chanting) ministers, honorable Senators, Representatives of the people, honorable guests and all other departing foreigners, gentlemen, and ladies; ladies and gentlemen, peace of Allah be upon you all. Before I go ahead, let us welcome Chief Justice Mohamed Ahmed Aburanat. Aburanat shall act as Governor General in this transitional period up to the time when he finishes establishing the Sovereign Council." (Intense applause and prolonged slogan chanting.)

The Prime Minister paused. The Deputies from the South all sat stiff-neck and grim. Minister Agundit seemed visibly tuned up with the Prime Minister and could clap. But, Deputy Dominic Muorwel, watching both the theatrical Prime Minister and Minister Agundit could not help but to express disgust and contempt for the two particularly Angundit, "He is just a stooge," he muttered. The Prime Minister started by lauding Deputy Abdel Rahman Dabka for his motion and said that he had the pleasure "to declare Sudan free and independent today," (There is immediate wild applause throughout the House, and among the crowd outside, South Sudanese MPs were silent.) The Prime Minister recounted the sad events which took place in Torit and the steps his government took to quash that mutiny and blamed subversive elements for having planted "the seeds of sedition among us" and those irresponsible elements for having carried out those wanted atrocities and promised severe punishment "for those found guilty and those who will fail to surrender." He continued:

> *It could not have been easy for us in this nascent government to contain the mutiny so quickly and so effectively had it not been for the deep understanding of Sir Alexander Knox Helm, our former Governor General, and his valiant assistant Sir James Robertson (He points to Sir James Robertson) Gentlemen and ladies. He stopped here and remarked, "We have one lady here, and laughed and everybody laughed. Then he continued. "Sir James is a man who has tirelessly extended help when we needed it; a man who has never spared a moment in the service of this country, day or night."*

He took off his reading glasses, glared for a while as if in admiration, and directly spoke to Sir Robertson; "Sir James, we should give you our Sudanese nationality, you deserve it," and swore in the name of Allah to confirm that he meant what he said, "Only it is unfortunate you are going to Nigeria. Stay with us Sir, can you?"

There was laughter and amusement across the Hall. Among those who expressed remarks of approval is Minister Agundit, while Minister Baluong is all smiles and some stomach shaking laughter. Deputy Wilson Andrago and Deputy Stanislaus Abdalla and a few other Deputies were contended with scornful smiles. Sir James Robertson looked around not knowing how to express his true feelings in this embarrassing situation; here is someone publicly offering him the Sudanese nationality for free.

> *Truly Sir, what you the British have done in this country, no other people could have done. True, I mean it (Sir Robertson grins while looking embarrassed, and there is humor all over the Hall.)*

Lazarus Dhieu extended his thin neck and enlarged his small eyes to find out what was causing this sudden humor. He looked at these two men next to him rapidly trading jokes, or whatever, their eyes bright with excitement. On the other side of the balcony, Lazarus caught sight of an overjoyed crowd unwound their turbans and waved them in the air with slogan chanting to cheer up that man with the big stomach; what on earth does he eat he is so fat like that, Lazarus wondered. After the interlude of humor, Al Azhari put on his reading glasses again and began to read his prepared speech in which he lauds the role Her Majesty's government played "to fulfill its obligations towards helping us to maintain our territorial integrity," and that now "the government has managed to crush the mutiny and has restored the functions of the government in that part of the country." The Prime Minister stressed he would like to extend a hand of peace,

> *to our brothers in the South through their representative here with us today, and together let us open a new page of brotherly understanding, to build this country.*

In his long speech, the Prime Minister mentioned that:

My dear countrymen, this may be an opportunity to make it clear to some citizens that we have carefully looked into the call for federalism, but we have found it unworkable and unacceptable..."

And he stressed that no one should make a mistake for "our iron fist shall swiftly and mercilessly come down upon any saboteur and any troublemaker (Applause and Allahu Akbar chanting continues for a while.)

Some Southern Deputies noticed that Deputy Celestino Awan was smiling in a way that can be interpreted as someone tunning up with the Prime Minister, was it admiration or was it out of a habit, none could tell.

The Prime Minister continued his rhetoric amid applause until he came to touch upon relations with the neighboring countries by thanking the governments of Kenya and Uganda "for having closed their borders in the face of the mutineers," and assured them of good neighborliness and respect for their territorial integrity. Concerning relations with Egypt, the Prime Minister assured that "relations are eternal as the Nile," and that "mechanisms of unity between our two countries shall be set in motion soon after independence," and reminded that within the few coming days they shall hoist the flag of independence up into the sky, "a symbol of our freedom among free nations of the world," (Intense applause and a prolong slogan chanting.)

Suddenly the Prime Minister went hysterical and with him nearly the whole House except those few Deputies from the South and with them was Lazarus who was bewildered by the events. Poor Lazarus could not understand what was going on, Lazarus may not know, but he was there that day as an eyewitness, watching history in the make. The Prime Minister's voice was still in the sky and emotions were still flowing, and suddenly, the man turned poetical:

> *Oh, sweet breeze of freedom*
> *I feel thee,*
> *Oh, soft melody of liberty*
> *I hear thee,*
> *Precious fruit of struggle,*
> *Tightly to my chest let me hold thee,*
> *Come…thou …come into my heart,*

And there to embrace thee,
Let me feel thee,
Come…come ye precious thing,
Quench my thirst for more…

The whole house went wild in applause and slogan chanting which went on for some time. Meanwhile Speaker Abdallah Surur made some futile attempts to restore calm. At last, the Prime Minister found chance to go on:

My, my dear countrymen, my dear, my dear countrymen, gentlemen, and ladies, in fulfilment of the noble dream of a great Arab poet this great historic occasion has just conjured up, let us recite with the poet:

Once a people resolve to be free,
Fate should give in,
And night should give way to daybreak,
And the chains of bondage should break lose

He was immediately cut short with loud, emotional slogan chanting from the crowd, which went on for some time, and tears from many eyes began to roll down. Overwhelmed, the Prime Minister stopped to let the crowd and the Joint House to express their emotions. Meanwhile Al Azhari took his handkerchief out to wipe tears flowing down his cheeks and blew his nose clean. Lazarus observed many handkerchiefs wiping tears and many noses blown clean. Some of the British and the Egyptians colonial officials seemed bewildered at what was happening; "My God," Janet is bewildered. Having recomposed, and the House quiet again, the Prime Minister continued his speech. This time his tone was lower though loaded with emotions. He emphasized that with the dawn of independence, Sudan shall join the Arab League, "Where fate awaits to play our role in the struggle against Zionism, imperialism and other reactionary forces in the region," and that they are going to form a transitional government that will enable them cope with the developments of the post-independence period, and that independence ceremonies shall be arranged as soon as possible and bade farewell to Sir Alexander Knox Helm and Sir James Robertson. Wilson Andrago, who was amazed, whispered to Dominic "Independence, is he serious!"

The Joint House erupted into a long continuous standing ovation, noisy slogan chanting including Minister David Angundit, the other two Ministers, and MP Celestino Awan, perhaps. The Southern Members of Parliament and those from the Black Bloc were the only people who did not join in all this frenzy slogan chanting according to Lazarus. All grouped in their section, some of them remained seated some rose but all looked depressed and stone face.

As Ismail Al Azhari returned to his seat. The British and the Egyptian colonial officials rose to receive the Prime Minister and gripped hands, starting with Sir Alexander Helm, Sir James Robertson, and the rest as far as he could reach, then raised his short thick hands up to the audience in the Hall and up to those on the balcony.

Lazarus could see that MP Celestino Awan and the three Ministers from the South stood up with the rest in the Hall. Minister David Angundit was seen enthusiastic and could repeat a slogan whenever he can, and Wani and Baluong were just smiling. Lazarus was watching all this and wondered.

As the standing ovation continued, MP Dominic Muorwel could not stand it. He rose and started to walk out. On his way out, he was immediately followed by Father Saturnino O'hore, Deputy Wilson Andrago and soon the rest of the MPs including Celestino Awan who immediately realized what was happening, and Lazarus who found an opening, all walked out of the Hall. Left behind were the three Southern Sudanese Ministers.

CHAPTER SIX

Yes, Arabs Are Not Good

Early in the morning, Deputy Dominic Muorwel woke Lazarus up, gave him money and ordered him to run and bring the newspapers, especially *The Sudan Standard*. Within a short time, Lazarus brought the three newspapers. Dominic threw the two Arabic papers on the small table in front of him and began to prepare himself to read the only weekly English newspaper recently published.

From over the fence, Dominic could clearly hear his neighbor's radio loudly broadcasting the recorded speech of the Prime Minister. Ignoring the radio Dominic read the headlines: "Sudan is Declared Independent; Ceremonies will Proceed as Scheduled," "PM Al Azhari Lauds Her Majesty's Government for Independence" and he read the story. Another headline provoked him; "Federalism Denounced," and he read the report through. He then opened the pages one by one up to the back page, "It can't be!" Again, he went through the pages giving each a good search, "What is this; there is no mention about our speeches, or our walkout, why? What about the strong balanced speech of Father Saturnino? Although he felt bad, Deputy Dominic continued to read, giving the Arabic papers a glance from time to time.

While the radio in the neighbor's house was still blasting out the speech of the Prime Minister, Deputy Dominic shivered, "It is cold," he complained. He got up and entered the room. After a short while he emerged with a jacket over the pajamas and sat on a chair under the verandah. "It is better, why is it so cold like this, it makes people look miserable. This wind is too harsh." The door of the salon remained locked.

Sleeping in the salon are some six of his male dependents including Lazarus who had gone under the bedsheet and resumed sleep. In the next room there are three female dependents, two are his younger sisters, Yom and Yar. Adut, a distant cousin, arrived here complaining of an acute abdominal pain and this has forced her to be selective on food and as a result she is as thin as a reed. Two months ago, her husband sent her to Khartoum for medical treatment and entrusted her to the care of her maternal relative MP Dominic Muorwel, who is now an influential person in the government as commonly assumed back home.

Just a few feet away, wedged into a corner of the verandah, lies Malow in a ring shape tightly wrapped up under the blanket because of the cold. Five days ago, Malow who is a distant uncle, was led by a nephew to this house during Dominic's absence. He too, is sick. He is complaining from a combination of ailments, the most serious of which are the chest pain and vomiting. Though he violently coughs from time to time, Malow is soundly asleep. It is not yet seven O'clock in the morning, "Next Sunday or Monday I will take them to the doctor," Dominic runs a thought almost you could see his lips move, "both need special food…no, the most important thing now is treatment, they should get treated first, they may think I have neglected them."

The Prime Minister is still blasting away in the neighbor's radio, "Where is tea, it is getting late," the Deputy started to be impatient and would glance at his watch. The slogan chanting and the applause from the radio were disturbing and caused more anxiety. Dominic could hear an Arab female's voice over the fence calling for somebody or for something "Northerners, Arabs; what can I do?" Dominic was trying to figure things out. Coming back from this morning mental roaming, his eyes fall on the Arabic newspapers, "Arabs; Arabic is not only complicated, but it is strange and very complicated just as they are. Look at it; see how it is written," his eyes are fixed on the papers, "from right to left, it is like driving against the traffic."

Morning tea is not yet forthcoming and none of the young boys was awake. Dominic's train of thoughts is still on the move, "Hear Arabs speak, some of the words are reached for far down the throat one would choke up; why? The neighbor's radio was just against the dividing wall its sound was making real noise. Tea was not yet ready, and Dominic was trying to keep focused in this seemingly cold morning weather but, "I think I should buy a radio, a reasonable one. How much does it cost? A radio is important, very important. I want to listen to the BBC." Then he picked up The Sudan Standard again and tried to read and then, "The English are funny; they mixed us up with people like these; how are we going to fare with them eh," Deputy Dominic wondered.

Suddenly Dominic looked at his watch, "Noooo, nonono too much; Machar, Machar, Lazarus," he shouted at the boys to wake up. Getting no answer, he opened the door of the salon noisily and everybody was still soundly asleep; some were even snoring, but all coiled under bedsheets. Machar and someone else are sleeping on the ground for lack of beds. Dominic stood over Machar and began to call "Machar wake up," no response. He came closer and stood right over Machar's head and called out louder, "Machar, Machar wake up." Then he reached down and shook Machar who was tightly wrapped up in a bed sheet. Again, Dominic came down upon him, "Machar get up it is broad daylight, get up what kind of sleep is this, is it not death, get up," all this in the native language.

Machar uncovered his head, opened one eye to see who is disturbing his peace then rolled over on the other side to resume his sweet sleep. Dominic came down on him again, and with more vigor he shook him awake. Machar gave up the fight and unwound the bed sheet and stretched while still on the mattress on the ground, "Get up," Dominic demanded. Machar finally sat up straight, rubbed his eyes and then yawned.

Dominic: Get up and prepare yourself, there is something I want you to do for me.

As a result of the commotion the rest of the boys began to wake up. Dominic returned to his seat and soon Yar came in politely with a tray containing morning tea. She placed it on the small dining table nearby and disappeared. She reappeared with another tray full of bread, then she poured milk and tea into one cup, then turned to the small table, pushed the papers slightly to one side for space and then she carefully put the cup of tea on it in front of her elder brother. And as she prepared to withdraw, Dominic enquired about the condition of Adut.

Yar: Same as yesterday.

Dominic: Does she eat, or is she still selective?

Yar: She eats very little.

Dominic: I will take her to a doctor very soon. Problem is, I don't have time.

He scratched his head and the chest and the thighs again and again not knowing what to do or what to say while the girl was standing stiff with her head shied away.

Yar: The way I see it, Adut is suffering greatly.

Dominic: I know, I know (The young girl withdrew) What can I do now, what can I do.

Malow: Muorwel (His voice came in from under the blanket) when are you going to pay attention to me, son of my brother.?

Dominic: This is what we have just been discussing with this little girl, but time Malondit, time is my problem (He silently repeated time twice or three times while shaking his legs; the weather was cold.)

Malow: These little girls have been kind to me since I came to your house; why don't you marry?

Dominic: Marry, what is missing now?

Malow: Why do you speak like that son of my brother? (He partly uncovered his head.)

Dominic: The girls do all that is needed, don't they?

Malow: No, that is not enough, the world is never known.

Dominic: You are right absolutely Atuungdiet. But right

now, marriage is not my main concern. The main problem is how to deal with these Arabs.

Malow: What Arabs? Do they prevent someone from marrying?

Dominic: (Trying to be humorous) That is not the case, Atuungdiet; that is not the case.

Malow is now sitting upright but still wrapped up in the blanket and began to cough. He too was trying to be humorous. There was some dusty wind blowing. Deputy Dominic was also holding the jacket tight round him. Time was passing and the neighbor's radio was still broadcasting the Prime Minister's speech. "Are you not still entertaining the idea of the priests, their habit that they don't marry?"

Dominic: No, no, that is not the case, uncle no; the fact is…that….

As this little discussion was taking place, Dominic took his tea while munching a large piece of fresh bread. Machar entered and started to prepare a cup of tea for himself, Lazarus appeared, and a second cup is prepared.

Dominic requested the boy to run quickly and urge Yar to bring hot porridge to uncle Atuungdiet. Soon the rest of the young men joined the party round the small table to take tea and eat this fresh bread with its nice morning smell.

Dominic: You, young people sleep too much, look at the sun.

Machar: It is too cold.

Malou: In the town young men do not count very much these days, don't you know that?

Machar: This is not true, uncle Malondit.

Dominic: When we were of this age (Pointing at Lazarus and another boy on the table) we would get up at dawn, milk the cows, clean the ground from dung and herd the cattle to the grazing ground, don't you know that?

Machar: (Showing a thick black upper gum and white teeth while grinning) We also have our assignments, a lot of things to do.

Malow: Here in the town? (Coughed)

A relative: Yes, uncle.

Machar: (Still grinning) We report to work very early, don't you know that?

Lazarus: (Also grinning) Like going to school.

Another relative: (Also grinning) Schools yes, uncle Atuungdiet. People are not just idle in the towns as you may thing. All people here in Khartoum and Omdurman start off to work very early in the morning.

Dominic: Of course, there are a lot of things done in the town. But your uncle means he does not see you active, you know, like young men of your age, there at home (Giving a big smile of triumph over Machar and the rest.)

While this conversation was going on under the verandah the Prime Minister was shrieking in the neighbor's radio which aroused Malow's curiosity "Why is this man shouting so loudly like that early in the morning, who is he?"

Machar: (Still grinning and exposing his black gum and white teeth) This is the Prime Minister of the country called Sudan, speaking on the radio.

Malow: But why is he shouting like that? (Some cough.)

Dominic: This shouting is a speech he delivered in front of us yesterday in Parliament.

Lazarus: I saw the man who is speaking yesterday, (Pointing towards the radio) He is very big, very fat. I don't know what he eats he is so fat like that. He was crying yesterday.

Dominic: He was not crying, this is politics, he wanted to win support only.

Lazarus: I was surprised, I saw others crying also.

Dominic: Do not believe that this is all nonsense. It's an Arab game to win support.

Lazarus: There was that man, I think he is from the South, he was very happy.

Dominic: This is one of the people who are working against us, we black people.

Malow: How can one do that?

Dominic: This man's name is David Angundit and he is siding with the Arabs against us.

Malow: Why would he do that?

Dominic: That is why you see me going out daily to meet some of my colleagues from the South to work together to stop him and others like him.

Malow: Angundit! People with names like that are not good.

Dominic: This is the problem we have found ourselves in, Uncle. Now with independence, if we are not careful, the Arabs will not allow us to live in peace

Malow: What will be good if the white man has decided to leave? What peace? Let them celebrate.

Machar: This is independence. I have heard about it all

over the town. All the Arabs are very happy.

Lazarus: Why are they happy?

Machar: Because it is independence.

A relative: What is independence?

Machar: (Still grinning and munching bread) to be free from the British and Egypt.

Malow: White men are staying in our country in peace, will they also leave?

Machar: Of course, they will leave, or they may have already left by now.

Malow: But they do not do anything bad. I have never seen or heard anyone of them killing someone or taking someone's wife or anything of the sort.

Dominic: Atuungdiet, we have a problem here and that is why you see me going out daily and come back home very late, and that is why you hear this man shouting since morning.

Machar: The Arabs have taken all the positions in the country, is this not true?

Dominic: That is not all they have done; they have gone to the South and have taken up all the positions the British have left for us.

Malow: Is this true really, how could they do that?

Dominic: Malondit, uncle, this is a very big issue. There was a fight in the South a few months ago, just before I arrived here.

Malow: A fight between whom and whom.

Dominic: Between our boys in the army and the Arabs.

Malow: This must be a very serious problem.

Dominic: It is. That is why you see these newspapers on the table. (Addressing Machar) Finish your tea and I want you to help me with these Arabic papers.

Machar was about twenty years old and was an employee in the American Textile Company recently established in Khartoum North. Like most of his colleagues in the textile mill, Machar attended evening classes and Arabic language was one of the subjects taught to them in the evenings at a Missionary School. Deputy Dominic Muorwel was lucky because Machar, who had spent about a year attending evening classes, can now fairly read and write Arabic. As soon as Machar finished taking tea, Dominic picked one Arabic newspaper and handed it to him.

Dominic: See what the Arabs have said, there is nothing in this paper, (Pointing at *The Sudan Standard*.)

Perching the newspaper on this small dining table, though he was used to reading in silence, Machar had his first oral test that morning. He was not only reading in a loud voice but interpreting it for his cousin and for the rest around the table. Machar had been in Khartoum since 1954 and he was proving that he did not waste that precious year in vain.

Pulling himself up closer against the table, Machar grinned as he read the first bold headlines from *Al Jalaa*, a highly popular daily: "Sudan is Free at last," then he turned to the next headline just under the first one that reads, "In a Tumultuous Historic Session of the Joint House, Al Azhari declares Sudan independent," and without looking at his cousin or waiting for his comment, Machar read another headline; "Elections to be held soon and an Interim Government Formed," and then read the story aloud and interpreted the gist of it in the native language.

Dominic: See if they have written about our walkout.

Machar probed the first page, the second and went on up to the back page. He went through the paper again turning the pages quickly. When he could not find anything relevant, again he ran his eyes through, page by page.

Dominic: Anything?

Machar: I am afraid there is nothing about your walkout.

Dominic: Okay, have they mentioned anything about the speech I gave?

Machar searched through the paper and in the end, he admitted that there was nothing of the sort.

Dominic: Okay, what about the speech of Father Saturnino and that of Wilson Andrago, have they been mentioned?

Machar: Saturnino-Saturnino (Machar probed the pages looking for Saturnino and Andrago. Machar ran his eyes again and again) No, there is nothing, no Father Saturnino or Andrago."

A relative: Who is Andrago?

Dominic: One of our MPs.

Apparently disappointed, nevertheless Dominic asked Machar to read the headlines.

Machar seemed exhausted because reading and interpreting classical Arabic became laborious. Nevertheless, he showed cooperation and patience; "This is *Al Shoa'ala,*" he announced loudly while leaning back.

Dominic: What?

Machar: *Al Shoa'ala* (He pronounced it slowly) if translated into our language it would mean something like light, or fire, something that gives light in the night.

Lazarus: What gives light other than the sun?

Machar: It is something that burns like fire…or a torch.

Dominic: A torch! I see, what does it say?

Machar held the newspaper tightly, "Aburanat is Governor General," and "Sudan is Declared Independent," and read the story while skipping some lines and paragraphs. Machar read another headline: "Sudan Joins the Group of Free Nations."

First Cousin: What is happening here, seems a serious matter.

Dominic: Arabs do not want us to join them to rule this country together. This is what it means.

Second Cousin: Why do you speak of ruling this country, are you an Arab?

Dominic: No, we are all Sudanese. I mean we the blacks are Sudanese, and the Arabs are also Sudanese. We are all Sudanese.

Second Cousin: What is Sudanese?

Machar: You don't know? Everybody in this country is a

Sudanese including yourself (Adding with a large grin and a chuckle showing that black gum and those white teeth) Even Malondit is a Sudanese, we are all Sudanese you know, it has just been said.

Second Cousin: Then what is the problem?

Dominic: I have just said, Arabs do not want us to join and rule Sudan together with them. They do not want us to be equal with them.

First Cousin: This can't be.

Second Cousin: Then why don't we leave them?

Dominic: It is not that simple.

Malow: Son of my brother, when will you take me to hospital?

Dominic: Soon as possible. Adut is also suffering very much.

Malow: Please try to spare time for me. I am suffering and then everyone in this house disappears during the day leaving me and Adut alone.

Dominic: I know (Scratching his head.)

Malow: Please try to spare some time for me and the daughter of your aunt.

Dominic: I know Atuungdiet, just be patient a little,

uncle (He turned to Machar while scratching his head and shoulders) So you say there is no mention of our walkout, all right, okay.

Machar: So far there is nothing written in these papers.

First Cousin: Why is it so serious a matter?

Dominic: That is why I am in Parliament to see that Arabs do not cheat us.

Second Cousin: If you speak of cheating, they have already cheated us. Look, wherever you go, you see nobody except Arab faces.

First Cousin: This is truly a problem.

Dominic: Machar, go and ask one of the girls to prepare warm water for me to take bath. It is getting late.

Dominic emerged from the bathroom which is some distance. The main house is composed of two bedrooms, a saloon, and a veranda. The verandah connects the two adjacent rooms with the salon. The kitchen is a few meters away from the main building, just in front of the girls' room which they use to spend time in when the veranda is occupied with men.

Deputy Dominic quickly walked into the veranda, pounded his wet slippers at the edge of the entrance to shake off the soil, and entered his room.

In the meantime, the neighbor's radio was still blasting out national songs while the two young men, Machar, and Lazarus, were still locking heads, reading the Arabic newspapers. The other two cousins had returned to bed to avoid cold. Deputy Dominic emerged from his room dressed up but without his coat. He carried a mirror and a comb and sat on a chair looking fresh but somber.

Before he finished combing his hair, Dominic inspected the veranda, now turned into a salon. There were four iron chairs with cotton stuffed cushions, six plastic chairs, some of which were used by the girls when there are no guests. There was a small dining table with four wooden chairs around it, a medium-size low wooden table and two other small side tables. There was no carpet on the floor, and no curtains. There was a large calendar with beautiful scenery and pictures hanging against the wall.

His distant uncle Malow Atuungdiet occupied that corner for lack of space in the salon proper, now turned into a room for the young men. Generally, Deputy Dominic would like to convince himself that his verandah was clean and not so poor, "but how long will I stay here anyway,"

Dominic would often reason, "This is Arab country." Against the wall hung several photographs, and there he is among fellow seminarians, all of whom are white. He appears dark but radiant in their midst with that big innocent African smile. All of them are in black robes and white cola. Dominic looks healthy and full of life, "Look at Calabrese, Giuseppe, a good friend. He is now a priest in Uganda. This American, Father Eugene taught me English. Look at me; mama-mia mama-mia." His eyes fell on the virgin kindly cuddling her baby. These two pictures have reminded him of Verona, and Padova, Milano, Ala, the mountains, fresh air. "It is now snowing" he muses his senses. "But there it would be crushingly cold outside and deliciously warm inside. Oh no, our rooms were poorly heated all the time. I was complaining and complaining, and they just laughed at me; Italians!" (Shook his head.)

As he sat there dusting his shoes, he began to hum "*Ave Ave Ave Maria*." Other Christmas carols kept coming into his head. Christmas is just five days away. Now in Italy, Christmas decorations and lights are everywhere, the atmosphere would be heavenly. Then his eyes settled on the picture of the Queen. They stared at each other for a moment, "The British, very strange people. they appear innocent; see Sir Robertson yesterday.

Yar entered to collect the empty porridge jug and the glass. On her way back to the kitchen, the jug in one hand, the glass-on-the tray in the other, this about matured girl posed for a moment and informed her brother that breakfast was being prepared.

Dominic: I am in a hurry; I am going to the town.

Yar: It is about ready.

Dominic: No, I have no appetite (Then adds somberly) do not forget your uncle Atuungdiet. You girls, dust the walls properly Christmas is approaching, eh? Machar help clean the corners up there and there eh okay. I am going downtown.

After these instructions Yar withdrew. Those on the verandah must have sensed a change in Dominic's mood which started right after reading the newspapers.

CHAPTER SEVEN

At the Central Station

Deputy Dominic arrived at the Central Station on Sirdar Street, which ran from Omdurman over the White Nile Bridge, passed through Khartoum City and on, over the Blue Nile Bridge into Khartoum North. The Central Station was a focal point in downtown Khartoum. Close by there was a newspaper kiosk and scores of shoe-shine boys, some were busy shining shoes and others were shuffling around their eyes fixed on shoes. Besides being a snack bar serving sandwiches and soft drinks, tea and coffee; beer and women are not allowed here.

Occupying a central position downtown Khartoum, the

Central Station was a point of convergence. Close to the Sirdar Street was a tram station and people disembarked and headed to their different destinations. Close by were the Taxi and bus terminals.

Besides reading newspapers and idling around, friends who had nowhere to go to, came here and socialize. If you have an appointment, here is the place. If you have no place to go to, just come here. If you have no work to do and do not know what to do or where to go, come to the Central Station. If you are bored or sleepy and would like to have more sleep, or would like to wake up, this is the right place. The Central Station was a place that was all inclusive; here were vagabonds, jobless, civil servants, journalists, lawyers, and politicians. The Central Station was a place where plain cloth informers and politicians rub shoulders, who cared, it's a free country.

From the Central Station wild rumors often originated and circulated about a real or imagined tension between the Umma Party and the National Unionist Party, about an impending showdown between the Communist and the Islamist student activists on the Campus of the University of Khartoum, speculations about the upcoming general elections and exaggerated accounts of an alleged coup attempt last week, who were involved and how it was aborted at the last moments. Hence, post-mutiny rumors still ran high here which alluded to "imperialist conspiracy" to separate the South from the North, or to "wide-scale massacres" of Northerners residing in the South; Arabs are very good at exaggerating, MP Stanislaus once said. Nevertheless, like the rest of the Sudanese, some South Sudanese vagabonds, jobless and politicians also found the Central Station a convenient place to idle in.

Before independence, many political activists were hauled from the Central Station and taken to jail. But today is a public holiday marking the occasion of the declaration of independence. This indicates that the Central Station will be a healthy place, a place convenient for socializing and refreshing. As a result, this place has never been so full like it is today.

Paying off the taxi, Deputy Muorwel walked towards the shade in long but firm strides, and before stepping into the shade he stopped, checked his watch, it was a few minutes pass nine in the morning. He stood erect to survey the area while smoothing down his long, blue-spotted necktie. Though the sun was bright, the weather was cold that morning, and there was some dust hanging in the air.

Deputy Dominic was handsome and youthful in mid-thirties. He was medium in height as well as in size. Having completed seminary in Verona, Italy and was ordained and remained a priest up to just last year, he resigned priesthood to contest elections. Today, he is counted one of the few well-educated in South Sudan. Besides Divinity, Philosophy, and other related subjects he had studied, Dominic was fluent in Italian, in addition to Latin and spoke good English all beside his native language. Although he received a full religious education in Europe and was ordained priest, Deputy Dominic was known of ill temper but tended to weigh things before bursting.

Dominic stood there for a few seconds, and then stepped under the shade. Before he could pull a chair which he found empty just in front of him, he stopped again to give one final sweeping survey. Anyway, by this time the place was already full of Arab faces and the big radio was very noisy here.

As Dominic stood while holding the chair with the copies of the newspapers tightly squeezed in the other hand, he caught sight of a fellow Southerner at the eastern side. Immediately he sported the chair and waded through to reach for him. They gripped hands firmly in a greeting at the background of smiles and very loud songs from the radio. Without introduction, Dominic put down the chair and both shared the table.

Young man: May I? (Pointing at the newspapers.)

Dominic handed him the English newspaper. This fellow Southerner was young, neatly dressed and in a nice-looking pullover and a tie. After a while this young man came back to ask "How are things eh?

Dominic: Not bad (Looking around and at faces.)

Young man: (Takes time to go through the newspaper) You are an MP, not so?

Dominic: Yes, I am (Still looking around, music is loud, and some winter dust is filling the air.)

The young man bent over the newspaper, page by page without reading a particular article. He folded the paper and addressed Dominic trying to make his voice heard over the blaring radio songs.

Young man: (Cynical) Sudan is independent now, eh?

Dominic: This is what they say (Looking around scanning faces.)

Young man: Arabs are happy, see them all over the place (He turns his head and this small trunk from side to side.)

Dominic: (Wryly) They have gained what they want.

Young man: You are right; see people like David Angundit and Alfred Wani, they are doing nothing to help their people.

Deputy Dominic kept quiet, and the young man picked the newspaper again and appeared to read a story, then came back slightly heard over the loud Arab voices and the big sound of the radio.

Young man: I think our people made a mistake in 1947 (Shaking his head sideways, then adds with bitterness) a big mistake.

Deputy Dominic felt provoked by this statement as it awakened sentiments which he had been trying to suppress all along. He too felt that the South had been betrayed but how, by whom and why, were his concerns. One of the reasons that compelled him to resign from priesthood was to contribute into the efforts to rescue the South, to liberate it from Arab domination. This young man has now brought those sentiments back, those dark memories of the infamous Juba Conference in June 1947.

Dominic: I also have the same feeling as yours. But what I know is that (Takes time to reflect) those who were brought to the Conference were promised posts (Again he stops to greet a new arrival who sits on a nearby chair and politely picks one Arabic newspaper to read) Besides, (Dominic continues looking left and right as if he is breaking a secret) the, the British also played us into a trick. They deceived our people that they will be protected by the government if the Arabs dishonor the agreement.

Young man: Not federalism.

Dominic: Yes.

Young man: Can't you people correct the mistake in Parliament, like to ask for self-determination, or...or...

Dominic: You speak of self-determination, look what they have already done. Yesterday, Wilson Andrago, Father Saturnino and I asked them to remember the main request of the South which is federation that should be implemented with independence together.

While the young man was waiting for Dominic to complete his elaboration, the newcomer was showing interest in their conversation and stopped reading to listen more attentively.

Young man: What happened?

Dominic: You see, the Prime Minister refused, isn't it written? (Pointing at the newcomer and to the newspaper.)

Newcomer: I heard the radio yesterday and this morning. It is terrible.

Young man: I do not know Arabic, what did they say?

Newcomer: (Getting warmed up) They were insulting Southerners badly, especially the poet. He was calling Southerners with very bad names you see, like imperialist lackeys and so on and so on. I mean, it is bad, very bad.

Young man: We Southerners are lackeys, or they who are lackeys!

Newcomer: He said that the Prime Minister should not listen to the Southerners, and even to kill them all.

Young man: Oh, noooo, no, nonono, this is too much.

Dominic: My cousin told me the same thing this morning. He read these Arabic newspapers before I came here.

Newcomer: Arabs are bad.

Dominic: So, this is so, okay, we shall see (He seems nervous.)

Newcomer: They say that the government is going to consider anyone who speaks of federation as a traitor.

Young man: Also, like that eh!

Dominic: Okay, we shall see (Trying to control his temper.)

Young man: How do they expect us to co-exist, eh?

Dominic: You know, when we knew that they were not going to listen to us, we had to march out in protest.

Newcomer: The radio announcer mentioned that yesterday. He said some MPs from the South were leaving the Hall and then went on like nothing happened.

Dominic: Indeed, this is what he did, we shall see, we shall see (He is suppressing anger.)

Young man: It is strange then no mention was made about that in the newspapers this morning.

Newcomer: You MPs must pay attention.

Before the Newcomer could finish his statement, Dominic's eyes met those of Deputy Celestino Awan and Deputy Lupai. Both Deputies were armed with newspapers. Immediately Dominic sprang up and all were radiant with smiles, some exposing large white teeth, others have large red gums. They gripped and shook hands in a rapacious and vigorous manner that drew the attention of some nearby Arabs.

As they shook hands, Deputy Lupai would burst into laughter that drowned the high intermingling voices in this place. Immediately the young man lifted his chair and came over and sat next to Deputy Lupai who addressed the young man directly:

Lupai: You did not come the other day?

Young man: James dropped in unexpectedly as I was preparing to come.

Lupai: So, that is the case, eh…my friend…

Young man: You know Sukiri. He kept talking and talking until it was too late.

Lupai: Yes because I waited and waited till it was too late.

The two of them laughed and shook hands again and Lupai went on shaking his knees and squared his arms tightly over the pullover to keep warm. In the meantime, the others continued to converse.

Young man: Did you go there? (Winking and blinking and smiling broadly.)

Lupai: No, next time (Some laughter.)

Young man: Okay, okay (Some laughter.)

By now the Central Station has become full of people most of whom are carrying newspapers. The three deputies together with the other two young men, pooled their heads to discuss issues of their concern.

Deputy Dominic signaled the cafeteria attendant to come and told him to serve those with him. The two Deputies and the young man requested lemon and orange juice respectively, while the Newcomer asked for tea with milk. Deputy Dominic asked for a sandwich and a soft drink.

Broadly smiling and shaking his knees as usual, scratching, and soothing his round stomach in apparent delight, Lupai opted to address Dominic. In the meantime, the others continued to read newspapers and to have their sideline conversation but in a very simple English, grammar and vocabulary are not an issue.

Lupai: How do you do, brother?

Dominic: Well, actually not happy, but not so bad.

Lupai: No, you are well, actually very well (Bursts into laughter.)

Dominic: Is there anything good here to make one happy, really?

Celestino: Exactly, you are right, the situation, the situation.

Lupai: It is exactly, see the weather, how cold.

Celestino: Exactly, not just cold, too much.

Young man: I don't know how they endure it. I am suffering all the time.

Lupai: You also feel the cold in the dormitories?

Dominic: Dormitories, which ones?

Lupai: University.

Dominic: This young man is a student!

Lupai: You don't know he is?

Dominic: Not exactly.

Young man: In fact, we have been here together but did not introduce each other. But I know you already.

Lupai: Brother, this is Alex Suleiman Duku; Katuum University-Law. He is my cousin. I am Lupai Taban Duku, you see. We come from Jebel Lado (Bursts into laughter.)

Dominic: (Looking surprised) Indeed, you are brothers, and we have been sitting all this time not knowing each other well!

Lupai: This is our great leader (Smiling broadly and small laughter) MP Father Dominic Muorwel, he resigned from the Church, and he now is a politician. And this is our great brother and leader also MP Celestino Awan. What is the meaning of Awan? (Awan smiles away with a broad smile.)

Father Dominic Muorwel protested that he did not resign from the Church but has chosen to try politics because, in his opinion, the situation is really bad and would like to do something with these Arabs. Having finished introducing themselves they all turned to the new arrival for identity.

Newcomer: (Rolls the newspaper tightly) I am Mordecai Mabor, myself and two of my colleagues are the first cadets in the Police College.

Lupai: Where is this, College?

Mordecai: It is near to Burri, close to the Blue Nile.

Lupai: I see, I see. I have a young brother, he finished Rumbek last year, can they accept him?

Mordecai: You bring a strong recommendation from a minister like Alfred, or someone, then he may be accepted.

Lupai: This is going to be difficult.

Celestino: Why? Just speak to Alfred and he will write a small note to the Commander of the College, or to the Minister of the Interior himself. Alfred know him, they are colleagues.

Lupai: I don't want someone to step into this.

Dominic: I agree with you. Let the boy apply on his own.

Celestino: Not the Police College my friend, that is very very difficult to enter.

Lupai: Anyway, I shall allow the young man to apply when time come.

Refreshments and the sandwich brough and consumed, the three Deputies brought their heads closer again to discuss a broad range of political issues. Among others, they discussed at length the impending independence ceremonies and what it meant as the British have already started to depart. Then they turned their attention to the events of yesterday. For Deputy Dominic, the media which was bias and discriminatory by all accounts in his opinion, was one of the problems to be added to the existing issues worthy of discussion.

Dominic: Why, why are Arabs so discriminatory like this? This morning papers did not mention anything about our speeches and walkout at least (Looking upset.)

Lupai: What do Arabs know.

Celestino Awan: The British Parliament is the real Parliament. There each member opinion and, and his ideas are respected and reported fully.

Alex: That is real democracy, not like ours.

Lupai: Yes, democracy in the real meaning.

Mordecai: Do you think, Mr. Celestino, we can call for the British to stay with us in the South?

Celestino: I don't know, can it be? (Turns to Dominic and Alex cuts him short.)

Alex: It would be a good idea, really.

Lupai: As far as I know, this cannot happen anymore, because Sudan has already become independent and the Northerners will not accept that one also, not so? (Looking at Dominic.)

Dominic: Yes, this is what I wanted to say. Now, we in the South have no right to ask the British to remain with us and they leave the North. This problem was discussed before, even the British will not accept it because they consider the North and the South as one.

Lupai: Brother Dominic is right. You see, Sudan is now independent okay, then you cannot go and ask the same British to stay in one part of the same country again, you see.

Alex: Is this country one now?

Dominic: This is our problem, you see.

Lupai: Yah, this is our problem my friend, you see.

Mordecai: You see, you the MPs, try to find us a solution.

Lupai: We are now fighting tooth and nail, my friend, it is not easy, you see.

Celestino: Not these Arabs my friend, you see.

While this discussion continued, the cafeteria boy swept by amidst deafening radio songs, collecting both money and empty glasses and cleaning the tables and rearranging chairs for the incoming new clients. Dominic paid him off.

After a short while, Mordecai asked for permission to leave for the Police College because it was time to report. The rest continued with their conversation on other subjects of interest. Dominic then reminded his colleagues about their appointment with Wilson Andrago.

CHAPTER EIGHT

At Andrago's House

The three Members of Parliament walked down Sirdar Street, shoulder to shoulder despite the crowds and traffic, heads bowed to the ground buried in some political discussion. A tram arrived and offloaded commuters. A taxi driver approached the three gentlemen offering his services and Lupai waved him away telling him, "We are going here, here," pointing just ahead of him.

As they stepped into San James Hotel, Andrago immediately signaled, and they walked towards him. Sitting with Andrago are Deputy Stanislaus Abdalla and Deputy Marko, all in coats and ties. As they have just arrived, they had not yet ordered for services.

After warm greetings and well wishes, they all sat down. Beer is brought and a light conversation ensued. However, the gentlemen agreed on the proposed meeting to be held in Wilson's house this evening in Sejjana, and that two other Deputies, Gatluak and Father Saturnino to be informed.

While sipping beer to the Western music playing in the background, the Southern MPs were suddenly approached by an apparently admiring Northern Sudanese who greeted them in very simple English; "Ooooh good my friends, you from South no, you South? (The man seemed extremely excited to meet these Southerners and was talking to them in English. He then hurriedly added with big smiles) Siidi Al Mirghani love South very much, Siidi Al Mirghani love South very very much," and before the bewildered MPs could understand what the man was talking about, this kind South-loving Northerner called for the bar attendant and ordered him to serve these Southerners with "two beer, two beer two beer," pointing at each of the six Southerners on this table and after that he insisted to shake hands with each one of them and then took permission to return to his table, apparently delighted. This small episode became a subject of an interesting interpretation and conversation;

"What did this mudukuru mean now eh?" enquired Andrago with astonishment. "You just come in and and and offer beer just like that!"

Stanislaus: He think we cannot buy beer for ourselves, or what?

Lupai: Arabs are very, very funny. See, somebody you don't even know just buy him beer just like that!

Stanislaus: And then he say, Siidi Al Mirghani or what, love you.

Wilson: Who is Siidi Mirghani? (Turning from face to face.)

Marko: I don't know this kind of thing.

Celestino: This is their way of life, I think. I saw something like this in the house of Minister David Angundit. They bring him some gifts like food, sometimes money (Small laughter.)

Dominic: Nonsense, Arab tactics to buy people.

Stanislaus: You are right, they can buy you in this way.

Deputy Dominic and Deputy Lual arrived at Wilson's house in the evening, and Lupai opened the main gate to check, and there he burst into laughter and welcomed the two gentlemen and led them into the salon to be warmly welcomed by Wilson Andrago. Everyone got seated and Lual opted to sit a distance from the rest.

Conversation was now on the weather in Europe and how severely cold it is by this time, and this gave Father Dominic a chance to relate some of his experiences with winter when he was in Europe, how sever it is, and the snow, the blister, and the rains and so on. Padre Domenico took time to explain what snow is and what blister is and what harm they can do. This prompted Deputy Lupai to remark that he cannot stand it, "Me, I will die with cold my friend, really," and a small laughter. But with a kind smile, Father Dominic assured him of all the precautions against winter, "Yes, my friend, not like ours here," Deputy Andrago, who seemed to understand some aspects of life in Europe, interceded.

On their arrival, Deputy Gatluak and Deputy Marko took their seats while this small conversation continued and this was a very interesting information to all, "But how how are the thethe the people in Europe there can live?" enquired Deputy Gatluak whose English is very modest for he did not have a formal education like some of the other Members of Parliament, besides he suffered stuttering. Then there is this strange weather in Northern Sudan; sometimes it is dusty, dry hot, and now it is cold and dry and windy and dusty, "It is confusing, you don't know which is which, or what is what," remarked Stanislaus. Lupai laughed and further elaborated on the point, and Gatluak added his interesting remarks.

While this small talk was on, Dominic took time to observe the salon. There are curtains and a large dining table placed on one side of the salon and eight home-made wooden chairs round it. There is a low wooden table in the middle and six smaller wooden tables used to serve tea. All the tables are covered with homemade embroidered tablecloths. There are six comfortable iron chairs covered with cotton-stuffed cushions and covered with colorful cloth. There is a small rug covering the floor under the chairs. Deputy Dominic's eyes fall on a radio situated at the corner, tuned to the BBC. There are a number of pictures hanging against the wall and a rather large picture of the Queen and that of King George VI. While Dominic was contemplating, Deputy Gatluak asked why the British appointed this small girl to become their Queen, "The thethe the King the King no boy?"

Stanislaus: Yes, did he really have a son?

Marko: I don't know. Maybe he has, or not?

Andrago: The English are like that my friend. They always appoint Queens. See Queen Victoria the the the First, and and Queen Victoria the Second, and and Queen Elizabeth the the First, and and Queen Elizabeth the Second; and Queen what and what I don't know."

Stanislaus: You are right, but why?

Lupai: The British are funny my friend, don't you know? (He laughs and is joined by Gatluak.)

Oblivious of what was going on around him, Father Dominic concluded that this salon is truly impressive by South Sudanese standards. However, in addition to the photographs of the Queen and her late father hanging against the wall, there are other photographs. Wilson's wedding photo attracted Gatluak's attention "Iiiiis this you and wife, Wilson?"

Wilson: Yes, my brother.

Gatluak: Wah, wah you look, you look very importan.

Lupai: How can he not, he is getting married, and his wife is next to him (Broad smile.)

Dominic was not distracted; here he is feeling

comfortable. Meanwhile, he observed four beds well covered under the veranda apparently for Wilson's dependents who had gone to the cinema this evening. Gatluak continued to pound Andrago with questions of personal nature, "What her name?"

Andrago: Dudu.

Gatluak: Dudu, yes, very good, very good.

In the meantime, someone asked about Christmas and the preparations.

Lupai: We shall make a party in my house.

Celestino: That is why you have already invited your brother there in the Central Station; you think I don't know? (Laughter.)

Lupai: (Smiling big) No, no it is open. Anyone can come, brother.

Celestino: Even me? (Big smile.)

Lupai: Yes, why not! Even you, brother. (Laughter.)

Celestino: Are you inviting me now?

Lupai: Yes, brother not you alone, everyone here is invited (Laughter.)

Dominic: Where is your home?

Lupai: Oh yes, I have moved to a place west of here.

Near the horse race filed you see, not far. There are neem trees there, and pots of water under the trees. (Pointing towards the direction.)

Celestino: Okay brother, I will come.

As they discussed plans for Christmas, a two-year-old boy appeared by the door well dressed, and hesitant, a thumb tugged against one cheek.

Lupai: Winston, Winston, come here; you want to be like your father or what? Come (He extended his arms to receive the boy. Winston is still standing by the door.)

Dominic: This is Wilson's son?

Lupai: Yes, his first-born. (He got up and led the child into the salon) Greet your uncle Celestino, and this is Stanislaus okay, eeeh yes.

The boy went on greeting each guest. He then reached his father who had been smiling all along. After a short while his father let him loose to send him for an errand

Andrago: Winston, go call mama.

Winston: Eeeeh?

Andrago: Mama, mama, go and call mama. eeeh.

Lupai got up and helped Winston toddle away and after a short while mama appeared at the door. Mama Dudu is young and is more beautiful than she does appear in the photograph according to Gatluak.

Andrago: Come in and meet these people.

Adrago reminded everyone that this is his wife. Dudu moved from one quest to the other, greeting each politely and Andrago invited his wife to sit and wait to be introduced formally to her guests. After a short while of socializing, mama Dudu took permission to leave.

Gatluak: (Surprised) This is your wife, Wilson Dudu in picture (Pointing to the photograph against the wall.)

Andrago: Yes, (Big smile.)

Gatluak: Very good, very good. I am now very very happy.

Within a few minutes, this beautifully dressed young girl came in carrying a large tray with tea, milk, home-baked cakes, cups, spoons, and the necessary requirements. Andrago immediately got up to help the girl. After the young girl and Andrago had placed the tray on the table, he introduced her to the guests.

Andrago: This girl is called Esther. Esther, greet your uncles (She begins to greet the guests politely one by one knee slightly bent.)

Lual: Is this your daughter?

Andrago: No, this is my elder brother's daughter.

Lupai: Not Scopas?

Andrago: Yes.

Stanislaus: Is she in school?

Andrago: In the Sisters' School.

Gatluak: Very good, very good.

Lual: Where is Sisters' School?

Stanislaus: You don't know; it is near the Cathedral, near the Blue Nile.

Lual: Yes, yes.

With the help of her uncle, Esther poured tea into each cup, some asked for more milk with tea, and this raised some interesting remarks such as "Why are you asking more milk, are you a Dinka?" and there was laughter. After cups of tea were placed in front of each guest, Esther withdrew and Winston toddled in again, wobbling towards his father.

Andrago: Gentlemen, the winter is cold, let us drink tea.

Lupai: You Dinka like milk too much, really too much (Pointing at Dominic and Celestino and a big smile.)

Marko: Why? Milk is our food (A big smile of pride.)

Gatluak: We, we also drink milk very very much. In my

country there, sometime, you can stay for a month even, with no food, only milk you see, only milk.

Andrago: Also, you?

Gatluak: Yes, my friend.

Lupai: Only milk, how?

Lual: Yes, My friend.

Stanislaus: Me, I cannot.

Gatluak: No, milk iiiss very very good to your body.

Lual: Lupai: Milk alone with no food!

Marko: Milk alone there in the toch where the cows eat grass and they become fat, you, and the cows there alone, there is milk only.

Gatluak: There nothing like milk, my friend, milk iiiss very good for your body (Shaking his arms together in a show of good health and strength.)

A short while after, the conversation shifted to Arab cultural bias and Dominic expressed bitterness that he never expected to share a country with the Arabs, and that he was completely convinced that Arabs are racists and, as Southerners, they should work to separate from the Arabs.

Wilson: You are right. You see this radio of mine (Pointing at the radio close to his shoulder) is fixed to the

BBC, only BBC.

Marko: What about other Stations?

Wilson: Just BBC my brother (Both Lupai and Marko laugh and approve of it.)

Dominic: You are right.

Gatluak: You see, you see, BBC iiiss the station even to me.

Wilson: You just listen to the language?

Marko: And the news, the news is perfect.

Stanislaus: Yes, not like what the Arabs say here in the Radio of theirs whatwhat or, or whatwhat, I don't understand.

Sometime was spent on this subject while more tea was served to those who had finished the first round. Dominic made a gesture to speak. Andrago kindly led his son towards the door and told him to go to mama and returned to his seat; he lowered the sound of the radio until it is just faintly audible. Dominic started by expressing sorrow for the absence of Father Saturnino in this meeting. Then he explained the reason for this meeting and the issues at stake. Dominic sated that the British have already left, and the Arabs have already taken over everything, that they are the Governors, the District and Assistant District Commissioners all over the South, and they are in the market all over the South:

But all this is simple. We all remember what was said at the Juba Conference. Where is federalism now? Yesterday, we heard that there is no federalism, and if anyone speaks of it, he will be considered a traitor and even taken to jail; how can this happen, can we allow this to happen? Again, look at what the newspapers are doing and the Radio. They did not mention anything about us at all. Are we going to stay like that?

He stopped for a while. Deputy Wilson and Gatluak looked somber and Lupai kept on shaking his knees with his hands squared over his stomach, "I think we should do something before it is too late" Dominic concluded.

Stanislaus: Thank you brother Dominic. This small gathering of ours is to make us to think of what to do so as to face the Arabs. I, in fact, I agree with Dominic. It is true that our history with the Arabs show the Arabs are not good people; they don't keep their word at all, at all. They deceive us always, and when we complain what or what, at the time when the British themselves are the ones who gave us to them to rule (Pulls back to sit properly feeling disturbed.)

Andrago: (Raised his hand to speak) He thanked those in the salon "for this small meeting to make us think of what to do." He went on to elaborate:

> *I for one, I think that what our Northern brothers are doing to us is just too much, too much (He stops to control his temper then continues) Look, we started with fed fed federalism. Federalism was our first demand so as to share the ruling of this country of ours and they have been doing like this (zigzagging his hand) See Sudanization came, and they cheated us. They said what, they said we have no education and and and no experience to become what, governors, or even police officer in our Provinces. Who among them was born with education and experience? (He is getting heated up and so are the rest especially Gatluak) All we are asking is to rule ourselves in the South and and and to share with them the ruling of the country in the center, in the center like in America.*

> *This is federalism my brothers (He raises his voice) Concerning the newspapers; the newspapers are always against us we the Southerners. The Radio is doing the same thing. Now since I bought this radio of mine, I have never opened Omdurman Station of theirs, or what or what, may be one time or two times just to listen to what the Governor General has to say. No, what the Northerners are doing is too mush. Brothers I suggest that we see the Governor General immediately yes, see him now.*

Lual: "Why can't we see Al Azhari first?"

Andrago: No, he will not listen but will begin to tell us "ba'adain, ba'adain, and insha Allah or what or what, we have no time with "ba'adain" of theirs. Then we want to know the position of the British before they go.

Marko: If this is the case, then I totally agree with you.

Dominic: Let us be objective. Brother Wilson has suggested that we see the Governor General. He is now preparing to leave for England. He is just waiting to hand over to Chief Justice Mohamed Ahmed Aburanat who is going to hand over to the Sovereign Council now being formed of five members. And Sir James Robertson is leaving for Nigeria soon, you see.

Lual: They are forming the Council already?

Stanislaus: Yes, my friend, you don't know?

Gatluak: Council, council what?

Lupai: To rule this country, my friend.

Gatluak: Wah, to rule! (Shaking his head in disbelief.)

Marko: You see all these things are taking place; we should hurry up and meet with the government.

Lupai: We make appointment with the office of the Prime Minister then.

Lual: I am happy to listen to all the views now here (The Deputy is coming in to make some serious remarks and the salon falls quiet again):

> *You see, our problem with the Northerners is not easy. See what happened yesterday. We reminded them of federalism so that we in the South rule ourselves they refuse. Brothers let us concentrate here, let us concentrate here (Pointing these two long index fingers to the ground twice for emphasis with his head down, then continued) Myself*

> *I support the move to see the Prime Minister to discuss federalism, only. Federalism should be put in action in the South. Other problem like the newspaper and Radio will come in also. I think it will be good to try to see him quickly even before the Sovereign Council is form.*

Wilson: I always agree with Lual. You see, now the problem is very clear. We see the Prime Minister and we tell him his government should put federalism in action now, nownow. (Emphasizing by pointing to the ground with that short stiff index finger.)

Dominic: (Checks his watch) Brother Wilson, we are not disagreeing, we have already agreed to see the Prime Minister, the problem now is how are we going to see him and when, you see.

Lupai: Yes, I think we can see him tomorrow, if possible (He gets heated up) You see, you see, just tomorrow.

Lual: Meeting the Prime Minister is not easy, my friend. We have to make an appointment.

Gatluak: Also!

Celestino: Of course, my friend.

Lual: Even this may not succeed because he is always having appointments.

Dominic: Let us ask someone close to him to arrange for us an appointment.

Celestino: All right, I shall ask David tomorrow to help us. I know him very well.

Lual: Yes, David is very very close to him.

Dominic: Then he will tell us when he will be ready to see us, alright.

The idea is unanimously agreed upon. While opinions are further exchanged, Celestino Awan informed the gathering that he has heard news of the execution of the two rebel leaders First Lieutenant Albino Lako and Second Lieutenant Renaldo and a number of rebel soldiers have surrendered, some of them executed and others imprisoned.

Lupai: (Stopped shaking his knees and appeared surprised and serious) Really, when?

Celestino: You don't know, this was two days now, in Juba.

Lual: Didn't they say they will be protected.

Stanislaus: Protected, these Northerners.

Lupai: No, this cannot be accepted. Are you sure this was announced?

Marko: (Chuckling) My friend.

Lual: The Arabs are not to be trusted, not to be trusted at all.

Wilson: If they go on like this, this federalism will not be even enough for us yes. I tell you (His eyeballs are getting wider with anger.)

Lupai: (He too is getting angry) Nooo, people have just surrendered to you; you shoot them, or bring them to court?

Gatluak: Surrender, why fight.

Lupai: They were promised, you see, they were promised.

Dominic: It is all the British. The British cannot be trusted at all.

Andrago: These people will make me change my mind about them, this is not possible.

Marko: My friend, we are in trouble really.

Dominic: (Diverts attention to the main issue) You see, I want to suggest that our delegation should be composed of us here only.

Stanislaus: I agree.

Gatluak: Why?

Dominic: You know, things like this are sensitive, because

we do not know what may happen.

Stanislaus: You see.

Gatluak: I think more is better (Stammering and serious.)

Dominic: You see, usually small delegations come back with better results and also, we do not know how this man is going to talk to us, we are few, we can manage well.

Andrago: Okay brothers. I think we have agreed on what we are going to do. Only we must remain united in the face of these mundukurat, and the British also.

Member of Parliament Wilson Andrago and the rest of the Deputies ended their meeting looking serious and resolved more than ever.

CHAPTER NINE

He is a Fox

After days of fruitless efforts, the delegation of the South Sudanese Parliamentarians managed to win an appointment with the Prime Minister. At about eleven O'clock in the morning, the Prime Minister received his guests and ordered plenty of lemon and orange juice, karkadeh, tea, cold water and sweets. According to instructions, the young errand boy passed the box of candies around for each to pick whatever he wants. Deputy Dominic and other three declined. Then the boy placed a glass of lemon or orange juice and a glass of water in front of each person sitting around this new long shining table. Meanwhile, the

Prime Minister would rock with laughter on anything he said but drawing very little amusement except from David Angundit and perhaps from Celestino Awan who happened to sit close to Minister Agundit. The Prime Minister would occasionally pick up this new telephone to answer calls from well-wishers on the independence, and on total restoration of security in Southern Sudan.

Prime Minister: (Amid loud laughter and jokes) Thank you, thank you, of course, all of us are free, yes, this freedom is for all of us, yes, yes (bursts into laughter) No, it was a simple problem; so far losses are not so much, yes; what? Yes, yes, not as they talked about especially on the side of the civilians of the South (Looks at the Parliamentarians) Yes, thank you (Loud laughter) ba'adain, insha-Allah insha-Allah thank you.

Under that condition, some of the MPs were visibly restless while the reporter and the photographer smiled sheepishly in their corner. Finally, Ismael Al Azhari turned to his guests trying to impress them and, for the sake of formality, the proceedings were entirely conducted in Sudanese English with some Arabic. The Prime Minister used the traditional heavy Arab accent and the Southerners used very simple and rudimentary English recently learned, except MP Dominic, the reporter could easily discern the breaks and twists in grammar, who cares.

Al Azhari: Welcome gentlemen. (He beams at them) You must have heard the news. At last, our army has managed to restore security in the South just a few days ago, just before independence. It means we can all travel again by plane or by land, you see as Minister David is saying (Pointing at Angundit and Awan) to Malakal, Juba, Wau no problem, you see.

The Prime Minister burst into laughter and was joined by David Angundit. Celestino, who was sitting next to Minister Agundit, was betrayed by a big smile he let go and Andrago took note of that. However, many of the guests were not amused at all as expressed by their rigid faces and some untouched glasses of lemon or orange juice. "But one thing you have to understand is that" the Prime Minister is seriously addressing his audience in a serious manner and in serious English for all to understand:

The army, our army, did not do anything wrong. Don't listen to what the BBC or any Radio Station says. (He stopped to reflect, then continued) But Sergeant Modi or who? (Looked towards Minister David who nods affirmatively with a big smile) Thank Allah, thank Allah, he saved the situation.

Again, Deputy Dominic, Deputy Gatluak and Deputy Wilson perhaps took note that Deputy Celestino was unusually relaxed and seemed to enjoy what the Prime Minister was saying. Deputy Dominic began to nurture doubts, "This is very strange, very strange. Awan you; alright," Dominic began to confide his suspicions and doubts about Deputy Celestino's change of mode to himself. The Prime Minister resumed his briefing:

He is a true nationalist; do you know what he did? With a few soldiers from the South, of course, he managed to save the lives of some of our officers and our civilians in Torit and in Juba also. Yes, marvelous, isn't it? It could have been a very big disaster (Celestino nods affirmatively while smiling) To me this is a clear sign of unity of the South and the North eh, eh. Some people go about to say lies that Northerners have stepped into the shoes of the British to colonize the South eh eh, how can this happen eh eh?

David Angundit: This is not good at all, not good at all really (He stopped for a while and then he introduced the guests to the Prime Minister one by one and ended by introducing Celestino Awan):

"Celestino is my friend, my best friend you see, he is going soon to join the Party of His Excellency the Prime Minister, our Party. Sayyid Ismael Al Azhari is the great son of the Sudan and he struggle so much for our independen we are now enjoying. His Excellency was very very busy in the past few days trying to see what was going on in Torit and now security has return to all the South, you can see now he is very very happy. You have now the chance to talk to him and to discuss any problem with him.

Ismael Al Azhari: Very good, excuse me gentlemen, I want to talk to Mr. eer eer (David gave him the name) A'ah Sssalastino (Addressing Deputy Celestino Awan):

Very good Sssalastino. David gave me some idea about you some time ago you see. Congratulations you will be very happy in our Party, and together with David you will work for the unity of the Sudan. Gentlemen, you are all welcome again, the door of my office is open to you always. You are welcome any time. I am here to listen to you.

Throughout the speech of the Prime Minister, Deputy Dominic Muorwel has been sitting dumbfounded; is what he has just heard true really or is he dreaming, one of those bad dreams, or a nightmare perhaps! "Awan, Awan, Awan, no wonder they named you Awan. No, this is not true. I have known you for some time, you used to visit David because of that little girl in his house you ended up by joining the National Unionist Party! Okay we shall see. Okay, okay we shall see," (Nodding his head repeatedly.)

Deputy Dominic dropped those threats for the time

being and tried to clear his mind to concentrate on what was going on in the office. The Prime Minister finished his remarks and there was silence; the photographer and the reporter were alert and began to capture what was going on. The honorable Deputies waited for a while to give Dominic a chance to collect his pieces before addressing the Prime Minister. Deputy Lual gave a nudge against Dominic's knees, and he came back to himself. He started by thanking the Prime Minister while rocking to sit more firmly, and cleared his throat while giving Celestino an angry eye; he started:

> *Thank you, ahhemm ahhemm (Clearing his throat) thank you Prime Minister, for the chance you gave us to meet you. We have in fact very simple problems, and we hope that you will have time to listen to us.*

Deputy Dominic rocked from side to side and cleared his throat again and again as he looked somber. He was not comfortable at all. In the meantime, all attention was focused on him; from his colleagues who expected him to articulate well; he is a priest and therefore knows how to speak well; from the Prime Minister who may not expect high respect and friendliness from this group and particularly from this former priest who looks aggressive; from Minister David Angundit who knows his position in this group of Parliamentarians especially from Dominic who had given him hard time before, and he still remembers calling him "traitor" in front of many people, and from Celestino; Celestino who, up to a few minutes ago, was a strong comrade, one among the group, but now!

Celestino is looking at Deputy Dominic with apathy and cynicism "What are you going to do to me eh, what do you have to give to me, who are you Dominic, just a priest; what politics do you know." Such are thoughts running up and down in the head of Celestino the defector, the turn coat. "Look at his eyes, is he really serious, we shall see;" such are thoughts turning around in the head of Deputy Andrago. "It is impossible, no, this is not true; Celestino, Celestino with the Arabs just like that," Stanislaus's head is also spinning. In his silence Deputy Marko would not like to believe what he has just heard, "Noooo, nono we are finish. Look at him, Awan Awan, noooo." The Spokesman is not comfortable under this shocking situation and that is why he is wringing his hands over and over. At last:

> *Okay, eer eer Your Excellency eer eer, we have come here to represent the Black Bloc, eer eer to talk to you and discuss two or three issues. We, the Members of Parliament from the South are asking your government to implement federalism. (The Prime Minister's eyes and those of David Angundit suddenly widened) Federalism is what the people of the South demand and it is the policy of our Bloc. The second is the newspapers and the Radio coverage of our activities as Southerners. Mr. Prime Minister eer eer, we may not know how to read Arabic language, but we listen, and we can understand it (Spreading his hand over the silent audience) 'He is a real priest, look at him,' (Mused Minister David.)*

The Prime Minister appeared to be concentrating as he tried to get at what Dominic was driving at. In the meantime, some Deputies showed uneasiness especially Deputy

Andrago who began to feel that Dominic was shaken judging from the flow of his speech.

> *For example (Dominic took in some breath and gave a cynical smile) for example, for example we do not find in the newspapers anything about the South and Southerners, about our viewpoints whether in Parliament or not. The Radio is totally empty of our voice. Also…*

The Prime Minister cuts him short "Excuse me excuse me; do you mean that the newspapers do not cover your activities as Southerners?"

Lual: (Interrupts) Yes and the Radio also.

Prime Minister: How?

Lual: You see, Your Excellency, we see that the newspapers do not write anything we do or say, while they cover the actions of our Northern brothers in Parliament.

Prime Minister: I see.

Lual: For example, when you made your speech in Parliament in December, some of my brothers here stood up and they said something very importan, very importan, but this was not written in the newspapers and even the Radio, the Radio did noy say anything, you see....

Prime Minister: Which radio, you mean the BBC? (He asked sarcastically.)

Lual: No, Omdurman Radio.

Andrago: You see, Your Excellency, our main concern is federalism; federalism is our first demand. We want federalism in the South now. And then we also see that our voice is not heard by the general public. (Rounding his hands in the air and anger is showing on his face.)

Prime Minister: Very well (he is feeling tension and observes that passion is running high among his audience) my dear friends:

> *I think Northerners and Southerners are brothers, and there is no difference at all (Using both hands to calm down the situation and to punctuate and emphasize as necessary) I ask you not to allow yourselves to be carried away by the idea that Northerners are colonizing you, nooo, no no this is not true at all, you see. This is not good for the unity of the Sudan. (Took time to look around)*

Look at David and and and our brother here (He looked at David to supply him with the name of the man sitting next to him. David whispered 'Awan, Celestino Awan.' (The Prime Minister strains to capture the name) "Aah, aah, what, who? Ah yes, Ssalastino, excuse me my hearing is not very good like yours." (He burst into laughter.)

The Prime Minister is joined in laughter by David and Celestino, who shook his head, and nobody knew why; was it in admiration of the man who was showing humor, or was he sarcastic about the situation he had just found himself in. Look, the Prime Minister is joking and laughing while his colleagues are threatening; what can he do? The Prime Minister continued:

I am very happy, we are very happy to have you in our Party, this is unity, no? All of you are welcome in our Party you see (Rocks again and smiles big) Concerning federalism, federalism what is federalism? Federalism is a government that is divided into small, small governments, small, small

> *governments. This is not good in the Sudan now, it will put Sudan into danger; South in federation, west in federation and what and what not. This will put our country in danger. In the future yes, maybe we will implement federalism but now this is not workable, don't you think so Mr. David?*

Mr. David took time to elaborate on real and imagined dangers of federalism if practiced in the Sudan now but agreed with the Prime Minister that it could be implemented in the future.

Concerning the newspapers, the Prime Minister continued and emphasized that if the role of the newspapers is properly understood, a lot of misunderstanding is removed for they publish any story they like, "even those they don't like," and that:

> *The only English newspaper, I think The Sudan Standing or Standard, what is the name? (He is asking Minister David and the rest about the right title of the newspaper) it is very small and it publishes government activities, but I will speak to*

the Minister of Information and Social Affairs to see your views can be published no, no?

The Prime Minister told his audience that "Radio Omdurman is facing difficulties," and that they are planning to increase its broadcasting hours to "twenty-four hours in a day, like the BBC. You know BBC is broadcasting twenty-four hours in a day, no?" (He laughs while Mr. David is smiling big) "You see, we have a lot a head for us to do. This is a new government, no?"

Dominic: Your Excellency, we represent the South, and the people of the South ask for federalism, and we believe that federalism is not a danger to anyone. What minister David said is not true.

Andrago: If I remember well, you mentioned in the joint meeting last December that federalism is not workable, but now we come back to you again to ask for federalism, this is the demand of our people.

Stanislaus: Yes, federalism is our demand, now.

Marko: Federalism is very importan for us in the South.

Prime Minister: All you have said is good, but federation may not be implemented now my dears. But I say that if we stand together (Looking at Celestino Awan) we can implement federalism together, no?"

Dominic: Okay Mr. Prime Minister, we shall discuss federalism in the future, but we also want to know where is our voice on the Radio, I mean, we do not hear our songs on the Radio?

Prime Minister: Our problem is how to improve broadcast quality. We want to train technicians, and we have a number of them who will go to Egypt very soon, and some also will go to England to be trained. You see, broadcasting songs from the South is very important, but this needs preparation, and now there is no enough money, but insha Allah, all these problems will be solved very soon, especially after independence.

David: You see my brother Dominic (He is interlocking his fingers and trying to beam at some of the rigid faces of the Deputies) I think the Prime Minister has made himself very very clear on the point of the newspaper and....

Prime Minister: (Cuts him short) Don't worry, as I said insha Allah, insha Allah you see, insha Allah I will talk to the Minister of Information and Social Affairs, and insha Allah, I just say insha Allah eh, he will find a solution for you.

Dominic: Let us hope so. But Your Excellency, we would like you to consider the possibility of increasing the representation of the South in your new government.

Prime Minister: How, I don't understand (He laughs.)

Andrago: Yes, we feel that the South is terribly under-represented in your government.

Prime Minister: I don't know what makes you people think like that (He is beaming while looking from face to face and at David Angundit in search for sympathy, perhaps) Already you have three ministers, David is here is this not enough?

Lupai: Your Excellency, we mean that we need Southerners to be appointed into different positions like Northerners....

Stanislaus: Your Excellency your Excellency, during Sudanization we did not get enough government positions, you see.

Prime Minister: I think the reasons that led to the South to have few positions are still on, no? Let's be patient my dears.

Lual: You see your Excellency, if we wait can this not lead us into developmen not balance well in the future?

Prime Minister: No, that is why there is a government, it is the duty of the government to see that rights your rights, are preserved.

Andrago: (Cynically) I am afraid if we go on like this, we will find ourselves at the end of the day in the same square.

Prime Minister: (Looking at David with surprise trying to find out why are these Southerners pressing on him so hard today) You see, I don't know why some people are afraid (He turns to Wilson and to the rest trying to beam as much smile as possible into their faces and possibly into their hearts and minds) I said that your rights are preserved, and there is no need to worry at all. (He is looking at Angundit and Celestino Awan for support) Only when the South is stable and has reached a good level of education, shall you get all the posts you need, and the present government, and the next one and the next, all shall preserve your rights, you see (Pressing his hands now and then and looking tense. Faces of stone are still rigid except that of Deputy Celestino who appears relaxed and is sitting very close to Minister David) Is there anything more than that aah, aah, or what aah? (Looking at David and Celestino for confirmation.)

David: (Wringed his hands then turned to the Parliamentarians while glancing at Celestino close by) Sssilowly, sssilowly (Emphasizing with his left-hand fingers and this revealed a brand-new watch round his wrist and he is smiling broadly) sssilowly my brothers, you can get all what you want. Let us be patient. This Prime Minister, there is no one like him. He was sent to prison in the South in Torit by the British and he stayed there for a very long long time. And when he came out, he won independen for all of us. So, we in the South, we will get all our rights if we join hands with him, you see.

Prime Minister: (Apparently touched by Minister David's words and began to sound emotional) You see, I like Mr. David very very much because he understands. He is my best friend, by God, and I like you people of the South very much. We in the North like you very much very much. You see, Mr. Sss Ssa (Trying to remember Celestino's name by pointing at him, and David gave him the name) Yes, Ssalastino is going to become a minister very soon, insha Allah, all of you shall become ministers if you join our Party, insha Allah, God willing (Pointing at heaven) and laughs.

Dominic: (Showing disappointment) Gentlemen, I think our meeting is finished.

Prime Minister: Why? (Looking greatly surprised) why, what happened; let us talk.

Dominic: I think we have finished what we have come for Mr. Prime Minister.

Celestino: (Looking surprised and disturbed) What happened, brothers?

Dominic: (In an angry mood and with angry eyes he addressed Celestino in the native language) Why don't you shut up Awan, we will meet outside.

Prime Minister: (Spreading his short thick hands in their faces) Nooo, please please stay (He called upon the errand boy to supply more cold soft drinks and sweets. Then turned around) Brothers, you have not finished your cups of something cold, lemon juice you do not drink aah, you want karkade aah or…?

Lual: No, Prime Minister, we are satisfy (Anger is visible.)

Prime Minister: All right, all right (Trying to calm things down while beaming a big smile) All right, I hope to see you again soon. David, please bring these gentlemen to me next time. I am at your service. (He got up to bid them farewell.)

Outside the door of the office of the Prime Minister, the seven Deputies stood in an angry mood and started to stage a kind of protest.

Andrago: Nooooo, noooo this cannot be, Celestino to betray us!

Lual: He is a fox.

Lupai: He is a fox only!

Dominic: Let him come out, I will show him, this dog.

Meanwhile this dog, Mr. Celestino Awan who, up to a short while ago was a friend, comrade, a brother in soul and in all purposes, cause and aims, has just turned into a fox, a traitor, a turncoat, a dog; and a dog he must be taught a lesson, and this dog has decided not to come out. He has found himself a safe haven in the office of the Prime Minister near the warm shoulders of his newfound fried, minister David Angundit. From now on minister Agundit will be his mentor and protector, and who knows he could become a minister soon as the Prime Minister has just promised, and who doesn't want to become a minister.

Guard: What is happening, you people ah aaah, what is happening, ah? (He is approaching seriously.)

Dominic, who was serious and furious, got hold of the

guard with one firm hand while keeping the other ready. In the meantime, the other MPs surrounded the guard, while Lual struggled to free the guard from Dominic's grip. "You go in and call Celestino Awan, you understand, Celestino inside there go, go (Dominic ordered the guard partly in broken Arabic, partly in English and partly in his native language.)

With the help of Lual, the guard managed to free his hand forcefully from Dominic in this small scuffle just in front of the office of the Prime Minister "Let me go let me go," the guard is struggling to free his hands while trying to keep the hat from falling off. What do you want ah, what do you want ah?

Dominic: Go in and call Celestino, he is inside (Pointed at the Prime Minister's office.)

Guard: Okay, okay I will call him (The frightened policeman hurried away and slipped into the office of the Prime Minister.)

Some officials from the Council of Ministers who happened to be there, those in the foyer waiting to see the Prime Minister and those passing by, stopped to watch the scene going on under the verandah.

A short while, David emerged followed by the reporter and the photographer with the angry guard in the lead, "What is happening, what is wrong my brothers, eh tell me eh?" David is agitated as he enquired about the matter.

Andrago: We want that traitor (Fuming with anger.)

David: Who?

Lual: The dog called Celestino (In the native language.)

Stanislaus: (Shaking with anger) We want him out now nownownow (Pointing to the ground with short angry fingers.)

David: (Trying to look and behave as calm as possible) What is wrong with you, my brothers? I want to know what is wrong. Look at these people, they are looking at you in front of the office of the Prime Minister.

Marko: Angundit, we are grownups and andand and don't treat us like this.

David: (Calm as possible) My brothers, I know you are angry and unhappy but but what did Awan do?

Dominic: You are also implicated Angundit, Angundit you are also implicated (Pointing at David with burning fingers while shaking with anger.)

David: (Still calm as possible) In what, in what brothers?

(Turning round from one angry face to another angry face.)

Dominic: You misled Awan, and and and you have made him to join the Arabs in their Party.

Lupai: Yes.

Wilson: This is not good, this is completely shameful, David.

The short guard in short khaki uniform and skinny Ali Shummu the reporter both closely stood by, keenly watching all that was happening, while the photographer was doing his best to capture the rare event. David ordered the two of them to move a distance away; nevertheless, the photographer who continued to take pictures and the reporter were greatly alarmed.

The two men left behind in the office also felt the heat of the embarrassing situation. While the Prime Minister was looking after some of his affairs on the table pretending to be calm, Deputy Celestino Awan the dog, the fox, is hiding in the office of the Prime Minister and will wait till this storm is over, "These are fools," Awan is turning things over in his small head, "What politic do they know eh, what can they do to me eh eh? Jut fools."

Prime Minister: Ssalastino, your brothers are not happy,

don't worry, soon you will be a minister insha Allah, don't worry.

Celestino: I am not afraid Mr. Prime Minister they cannot do anything to me, I am not afraid.

Prime Minister: I will talk to David to find you a place to stay in don't worry Ssalastino. I will make you a minister, insha Allah, insha Allah…

Celestino: No worry, Mr. Prime Minister…I am not afraid (Some smile.)

The scuffle was still going on under the verandah with Minister David doing his utmost to contain it.

David: (Calm as possible) My brothers, Lual, Stanislaus (He is turning from one angry Deputy to the other in supplication and he is speaking to them partly in English and partly in the native language) Stanislaus, Lual, please listen to me, by behaving the way you are doing you bring shame to us black people….

Wilson: What shame? We are already in shame, we want Celestino…

David: Celestino case is finish.

Gatluak: Finish you youyou think how cancan-cancan (Not able to complete the sentence because of anger and stutter.)

Dominic: (Cuts Gatluak short with high emotions) You see, we have a problem with these Arabs, and we have agreed to stand together tototo toto to fight fofofofor for our people. Awan was with us he knows our policies, and you deceived him.

David: (He managed to pull them farther away from under the veranda of the office of the Prime Minister) I did not deceive him brother (Spreading his two clean fat hands in front of them in supplication) Awan want to deceive the Arabs by playing this game you see, don't you know, this iiiss politic, you think he do not know the problem no, he know, this is just politic.

Dominic: This is dirty politics, our people do not like this dirty sort of politics of yours…

David: (Calm as ever with some smile) My brothers, my brothers, give this man chance, give this man chance, maybe he can bring you something good…

Lupai (In an angry mood) Noooo, Celestino is finish, finish you see….

Gatluak: Good, good what.

Stanislaus: Yes, finish he is finish (He is hysterically emphatic.)

Wilson: Tell him, go and tell him, we do not want to see him again even if he become a minister.

Dominic: I wanted to beat him by God (Biting his finger in anger and determination.)

Lual: Let us go, these are useless people, let us go....

David: You see, standing here like this is not good, Marko, Gatluak look at all these people, please go....

Marko: Tell him we shall meet.

The seven Members of Parliament started to walk away in utter disgust and anger. The policeman walked them out at a distance while trying to avoid further provocation. Ali Shummu the reporter and the photographer were soon swarmed by the employees who were sightseeing the event.

Deputy Dominic Mourwel, Lual and Gatluak got down from the taxi and started to walk home in an apparent bad temper. The three men took liberty to speak in their native language and some Northerners standing by and those walking by wondered as to what has happened that these Southerners are yelling in the street. A neighbor, who happened to stand at the door of his fence, raised his hand to greet "ass-laam a'alaikum," but received no response. He raised his voice louder putting on a big smile for his neighbor and again he greeted "asss-laaamu a'alaikum, ya jama'a, itfadalu," again no response. Ignoring the neighbor, the three Deputies from the South were locked up in a heated discussion, with hands and neckties flying in the air. Gatluak drew attention to the greeting of the neighbor, but Lual rebuked him and told him not to mind.

Some young boys who were playing football along the street, stopped to watch these shouting Janubeyeen in amazement and kept watching until the Deputies entered the house.

Lual and Gatluak approached Malow who was sitting upright in bed, coughing from time to time. Malondit found a chance to explain his condition and indirectly complained of the difficulty of seeing a doctor. Dominic defended himself by assuring the two gentlemen that he will attend to Malondit within the coming few days. "We are busy, I am very busy."

As he was explaining Malow's ailment to his colleagues, and plans to let him get treated, and his alibi that he was very busy, Lazarus came in and greeted the two MPs with whom he was already familiar. Apparently in bad mood, Dominic instructed Lazarus to tell Yom or Yar to bring drinking water, quickly. Lazarus disappeared and returned and sat on a chair some distance away from the angry Members of Parliament who continued their heated discussion.

Soon Yar came in with a jar of water and glasses in a tray and put them on the dining table. She then filled the three glasses with water and placed each glass in front of each angry guest and before she withdrew, she whispered to her brother whether to prepare lunch.

After lunch, the three Deputies resumed their high tempered confabulation all over again to review the events of the day and tried to find an explanation for the dramatic defection of Deputy Celestino Awan. "… he is nothing but a greedy person, he has no principles," yelled Dominic, eyes getting closed because of anger. Uncle Malow Atuungdiet got aroused and enquired about the matter.

Lual: We are discussing our miserable condition, Atuungdiet.

Malow: What happened, eh what happened so bad like this?

Lual: The Arabs; they are showing us how bad they are.

Malow: What have they done to you?

Lual: Awan, you know him. The Arabs have made him to join their Party.

Malow (Coughing) What is wrong with that?

Lual: This is very bad; it undermines our efforts.

Lual: Didn't you hear the Prime Minister promising him a ministerial post?

Dominic: We are not here to look for ministerial posts, or money or anything like that. We Southerners want the Arabs to let us be free....

Malow: Then they should let us free.

Dominic: This is what Awan and Angundit want to prevent.

Gatluak: This David, what iisiis his problem eh?

Dominic: He is a traitor, just a traitor.

Lual: He has been bought by the Arabs....

Malow: Bought? A big man like that can also be bought.

Dominic: Arabs are playing dirty tricks on us, Atuungdiet, you see.

A short while later, the three Members of Parliament took a taxi and headed for the house of Wilson Andrago whom they found boiling with anger. Lual reminded him to dial Radio Omdurman because it was just about news time. The announcer began the lead: "His Excellency, the Prime Minister, met this morning with a delegation of the Members of Parliament, the Black Bloc, who came to congratulate his Excellency on the occasion of utter defeat of the mutineers and the return of tranquility to the precious part of our country." On hearing the news, Deputy Dominic shouted: "Did you hear that, we went for a purpose, and they are announcing something else!" Gatluak enquired about what happened and the story is explained to him.

Gatluak: Wah, wah wah, this what he say! Wah, wah wah! (He is extremely surprised and bewildered.)

Lual: Yes, my friend, yes.

Gatluak: (Biting his right-hand index finger an act of utter anger a ready-to-fight indication) Wah gaar, ifififif if wewee in our home, you see, wah, nothing to solve this only fight, you see, only fight, wah!!

Dominic: Of course, nothing can solve this but fighting…

Gatluak: Politic, politic what politic, politic not good with Arab only fight, fight….

Wilson: Nonono, we shall fight, not these Arabs, no we

shall fight (Wagging his short index finger) really, brother (Facing Lual and Gatluak) nononono, we shall fight.

Dominic: You are right. As I see it nothing will solve this problem except fighting....

The five Members of Parliament continued their heated discussion till late into the night on the background of Arab songs from Radio Omdurman, and this could probably be the first time any of these angry Deputies had ever heard Sudanese music.

CHAPTER TEN

This is life

It was November and the weather was cold dry and windy. This cold weather seemed to have revived some memories. In retrospect, Member of Parliament, Father Dominic Muorwel, apparently in bad mood, remembered one of his close MP colleagues had defected. That was an unnecessary move Awan did, Southerners in the Black Bloc needed to remain united to fight together to win their rights. They should do so because they were fighting a merciless malicious enemy, an enemy that does not know that he is an enemy, an enemy that enjoys both regional and international support. The enemy is a sovereign State, and this is not simple. The best weapon available and suitable against this kind of an enemy is solidarity; "Awan why, why did you do that, why did you join The National Unionist Party?" Dominic wanted to know.

How many a night had Dominic been up to very late in the night, praying and contemplating the reasons that can compel a person to abandon his creed so easily, "Was he not a politician, didn't he win the election, was he bought or was he deceiving the Arabs as minister Agundit confided?" Obviously, Dominic's mind was turning things over trying to find out the reasons and the justifications for such a sharp U turn.

MP Father Saturnino was equally depressed when news about the defection of MP Celestino Awan reached him, "Why did he do that, why eh; how can he explain that eh; it is terrible." Like Dominic, Father Saturnino seemed powerless to confront this new unexpected dramatic development, "Just who can believe that?" enquired the priest.

One night Dominic's uncle Malondit stopped breathing. Dominic thought that his uncle was quiet under the blanket because of the cold. Late in the afternoon, some of his relatives and MP colleagues came to pay their condolences,

"He had a long lung problem." Dominic kept repeating this for two or three days to those who came to pay their respects. In the end, he told them "C'est la vie" as the French would say in a situation like this. It is true, that's how life is.

However, it was a relief that Adut, this distant cousin, managed to return home. In the meantime, her bed has been occupied by others who have come and gone. Dominic has been observing faces of his dependents in the salon have also kept changing; some disappear, others appear.

One good thing, according to Dominic was that Lazarus was doing well at Comboni School, his grades were very good, and he was picking up Arabic, "Study well; may God bless you my son," he would assure himself. Likewise, his two sisters were also doing well at the Sisters' School. Nevertheless, many people and political developments were changing, and Dominic was aware, though not changing.

Since the beginning of November, the tempo of both Parliamentary and Senate sessions increased dramatically and so were the public rallies; the up to very late into the night meetings, some were secret, others were not. The Parties seemed to be in a race against time or against destiny. Mostly those meetings were on a double prong rail, the Black Bloc, composed of the Southern Sudan Parliamentary Members, and the General Union of the Nuba (GUN) and the Darfur Renaissance Front, all were resolved to push for a Bill in Parliament next week to enact federalism.

At the same time the Northern Opposition Parties, spearheaded by the Communist Party, were feverishly preparing to throw a vote of no confidence next week too. To a political observer, there was a very hot contest between these two groups; one pressing for federalism, and the other pressing to oust the present government.

Early in the morning, 17 November 1958, MP Dominic got up from sleep and completed his morning prayers. As he returned from the toilet, he felt that his neighbor's radio was playing martial music in an unusually high pitch. He entered his room and turned on the radio already fixed to the BBC. Soon the Big Ben signaled four O'clock Greenwich Mean Time, six O'clock local time, and then in an unusually dramatic tone typical of this proud Brit, this seasoned announcer started the lead; "There is a coup d'état in Sudan last night and the whereabouts of the Prime

Minister are unknown." In the subsequent details, the proud British announcer went on to mention that "the elected government of Prime Minister Abdalla Bek Khalil has been ousted in what seems to be a bloodless coup," and that the army under the command of General Ibrahim Pasha Abbud has taken over power, and that political parties have been banned, and that a curfew is imposed; "Whatwhat, what, a coup d'état, last night eh; how how is that!!!" The astounded Member of Parliament wanted to know.

News ended and this seasoned proud Brit repeated the lead once again confirming that indeed there was a change of system of government in Sudan last night, and that the army had taken over the reins of power and that no parties were allowed to function anymore, and that there was no movement in the streets till further notice.

Dominic came out from his room feeling a strong push of an invisible force to listen with a concentrated attention to his neighbor's radio which was announcing a statement in a firm, but hectic revolutionary tone. He immediately rushed into the salon and woke Lazarus up and told him to sit here and wait. Then he popped into his room and came out with the radio and tuned it to Radio Omdurman, "I want you to listen carefully and tell me what is happening okay, okay?"

Lazarus strained his delicate senses and could get that this is a statement from the authorities of the government that "there is no walking in the streets today, and that anybody found violating this order will be severely punished, that Parliament is closed and no Parties from now on, that the army is in full control of the situation, that…" "So, the BBC is correct there is a coup; a military takeover, okay okay," confirmed Dominic.

Dominic became sure that what he had heard over the BBC was confirmed by Radio Omdurman. Nevertheless, he gave money to the boy and ordered him to rush and fetch him any newspaper and the boy rushed out and soon came back gapping and reported that the kiosk was closed, and that there was no movement outside. Father Dominic was now double sure that the news from the BBC was confirmed correct.

By this time Radio Omdurman had return to playing Martial Music. Dominic redialed the BBC which was running sports news and waited patiently for the next hour newscast. Soon Martial Music stopped, and MP Dominic overheard the voice of the announcer over the Radio Omdurman in his neighbor's radio changed, he was sounding subdued. Again, Dominic redialed Radio Omdurman and ordered this little boy to help him by paying good attention to what was being said, "This is the leader of the army speaking," Lazarus relayed the information.

Dominic: Aah, has he mentioned his name?

Lazarus: Ibrahim Pasha Abbud, or something like that.

Dominic: Ibrahim, Ibrahim Pasha Abbud, it was mentioned by the BBC, okay pay attention. So, there is a change of government eh, (Dominic's train of thoughts is on the move) What shall I do, what do I do now; where is the Prime Minister now, what is he doing now, where is Wilson and Father Saturnino now, where is David Angundit now (Then turned to Lazarus) they say no one is to go out from his house, till when?

Lazarus: I don't know (Seeing his uncle perplexed, Lazarus is beginning to feel worried.)

Dominic: Okay, pay attention, they will announce it later.

Lazarus: What has happened?

Dominic: The army has taken over the government.

Lazarus: Why, will there be a fight?

Dominic: No, there will be no fighting, they just want to rule this country. They don't want civilians like me and Minister David Angundit to be in the government.

Lazarus: Where is Angundit now?

Dominic: I don't know.

Lazarus became more alarmed after having learned about this military takeover, and about the fate of minister Agundit and possibly about the fate of his uncle; otherwise, why is he worried, there is no one in the street, there are no newspapers as usual, and there are no open shops, this means that he will not go to school today.

Lazarus: Shall I go to school?

Dominic: Nooo, go and tell Yom and Yar not to go to school, go.

The fourth day, Father Dominic Muorwel managed to reach the Central Station on Al Jamhouria Street, for this is the new name given after independence in place of Sirdar Street. It was good that he could meet with Deputies Lupai, Gatluak and Stanislaus, but there were few shoeshine boys and fewer shoes to shine, and a small number of caterers who seemed to drag their feet, not quick to respond as they used to be just last week; definitely, this is a new era. But the radio in the Central Station was louder and noisier as it broadcast more announcements and repeated the same Martial Music and national songs.

In general, the situation was clam under the shade, however gathering was forbidden by law. Hence, those who managed to gather anywhere, not only here under the shade of the Central Station, must be sure they are few, their voices low as possible and their facial expressions should be as normal as possible, who knows, this is a Revolution.

Lupai: So, they made a coup, eh (Still shaking his legs and crossing his arms across his round stomach but with half the smile of a few days ago.)

Dominic: What do they call this now?

Stanislaus: Some Northerners call it "thawra" or what, meaning Revolution (Small chuckling.)

Dominic: Revolution, what do they know about revolutions; they just talk.

Lupai: You are right; they don't know anything, what Revolution (Low chuckling and small stomach shaking.)

As the three Deputies sat around a table and three cups of tea in front of them, Gatluak appeared and pulled a chair; there is not much problem to get a chair today. The Deputies greeted each other warmly and Lupai addressed Gatluak with the title of former MP, "how about it my friend," and they all laughed which almost drew attention and they soon realized that this was not appropriate, this is a Revolution.

The four former Members of Parliament arrived at San James to find former Members of Parliament Wilson Andrago and Lual sitting in a corner, and beer is on the table. The Arab customers sat near and far and some closely grouped. These groups were definitely concerned, for some of them would like to know how this Revolution happened. Others would like to know why the Revolution happened, others would like to know who were behind the coup and who were behind those behind the coup, and who were behind bars.

1st man: (In a low voice while looking around with these heavy glasses) It is all Egyptian conspiracy.

2nd man: (In a lower voice) No, it is British.

1st man: Egyptian, British the same, they are all the same, if you ask me.

3rd man: Leave all this, where is the Prime Minister?

1st man: (Eyes rolling around) I heard he is behind bars.

2nd man: No, he is under house arrest.

3rd man: What does that mean?

From his seat in their corner in this bar and observing what was going on in the other beer drinking corners, former MP Stanislaus uttered that Arabs are very good at speculating and analyzing, and by the way what happened to the Prime Minister and minister David Angundit was the question that concerned former Members of Parliament, the answer will show the way forward; are they recognized by the new government, will there be elections, will they be imprisoned as rumors suggested some of the Party leaders have already been rounded up and some of the ministers have been detained; where? The six former Members of Parliament agreed to proceed to Andrago's house and continue their sitting.

Mrs. Dudu served the gentlemen their favorite native recipe so dear to many a former Member of Parliament, especially those who were not married, and this prompted former Member of Parliament Stanislaus to remark that when his wife is not at home, he would miss this kind of food to which former Member of Parliament Padre

Domenico agreed, and that he often missed this delicious food because his two sisters spend the whole day at school, and often had no time to prepare it; "I feel happy when I am in your house my friend, Dudu knows how to cook really."

Gatluak: I like Wilson house bebe bebebe becau because Dudu cook very very good (Stuttering as usual but seems to be picking up English.)

This prompts Lupai and Stanislaus to laugh freely and to suggest to the former priest to marry, "or this is not allowed by the church?" asked Lupai.

Dominic: Normally when a priest abdicates, he is now free, he can marry and do other things, no problem.

Lual: What is "abdicate"?

Dominic: It means to resign, to give up, not be a priest anymore.

Andrago: But Father Saturnino is a priest and a politician, right?

Stanislaus: Yes because he did not resign, I understand, is it not like that?

Dominic: He did not resign but, he has some problems with the Church, you know; the church does not allow religion to be mixed with politics.

Lual: Why, what is wrong?

Dominic: This is a matter of doctrine; this a long story.

Lupai: Chaah, doctrine is a very big word!

Stans: This is a serious matter my friend, the church....

Lupai: Okay, now you are free, can you now marry, no problem?

Dominic: In my case I cannot say now that I am going to marry, and now there is no politics allowed…

Andrago: Yah politics, are we really going to be politicians again?

Gatluak: Pol, pol politic what, politic of Arab not good.

Stanislaus: Myself I will go home and see what I can do.

Gatluak: Iiif if if no fed fed federalism I fight, fight (Wagging his long index finger seriously as usual.)

Lupai: But will it be easy with this situation.

Gatluak: What easy, easy what go to bush and and fight (Throws his long arms into the air and anger is evident on his face.)

Dominic: My friend, this needs preparations and and a lot of things, you see.

Gatluak: In my home there no wait, we fight the Arab.

Andrago: I support my brother Gatluak. Now there in my home, in the village down there now, young men are now preparing to fight, nownownow now down there (Red eyes are shooting out.)

Dominic: No, actually we shall fight. But we want this new government to know that we are asking for federalism, if they refuse, we shall fight.

Gatluak: They not listen, my friend to tototo to you, not these Arabs, wah.

Lupai: (Stopped shaking his legs and appeared to be serious) No, if they don't listen, we shall fight; yes, (Eyes are turning red.)

In the meantime, former Member of Parliament Wilson Andrago tuned the radio dial to Radio Omdurman and there was a national song, and it was soon followed by a news cast from which the former Members of Parliament could understand that pursuant to previous announcements, curfew hours have been reduced and shall start from eight O'clock in the evening, and that the new government shall be announced tomorrow.

Lual: Is it true they are announcing the new government tomorrow?

Dominic: Let them, who cares

Wilson: Myself, I don't care.

While sitting in the warmth of Dudu's hospitality, these gentlemen would want to know what will become of them as former Members of Parliament, what will become of the former ministers, what will become of the South under the new revolutionary order, and what will become of federalism?

The former Members of Parliament concluded that it was too early to judge the book by the cover, and that it was better to give the new system time and then see what can be done. But the former MPs emphasized that if the new government fails to implement federalism, they will have no choice but to fight.

On November 25, 1958, Father Dominic Muorwel was listening to Radio Omdurman morning news cast, a habit he recently acquired, and here were the names of the ministers in the new cabinet. The announcer mentioned the names of the following ministers to represent the three respective Southern Provinces and they are: 1-Mr. David Angundit, 2-Mr. Gatluak Biliu, 3-Mr. Wilson Andrago, "My good God, impossible! Is it possible really! How can this happen! These Arabs appoint people just like that eh!" Father Dominic called Lazarus to help him understand and interpret Arabic; this strange and complicated language that is written in the opposite direction, just like driving a vehicle against the traffic flow as his uncle once thought.

The boy and his uncle spent two hours almost following up developments, "Have they appointed David again eh, have they appointed Gatluak and Andrago. But have they been consulted; why did they not inform me, eh?" Father Dominic's brains are at work trying to decipher this conundrum.

Later Lazarus handed him "Al Thawra" newspaper and there are the photos of his friends, "Yes, this is Wilson … this is Gatluak, I see," and Omdurman Radio is blaring national songs and Marital Music right on his table and this had never happened before.

Five days later, after the impact of the Revolution and formation of the new cabinet had subsided, Father Dominic took a taxi to reach the house of Minister Wilson Andrago but found the house empty. He was told that, three days ago, Wilson had moved to a new house in Ashara Biyuut, an exclusive neighborhood in Khartoum reserved for ministers and he was told how to reach it.

Soon the taxi halted in front of the house and Dominic approached the police standing guard. He identified himself and revealed the purpose of his visit. He was told to wait for a while under the tree with the others because his Excellency was receiving guests and well-wishers. At last.

Dominic: Congratulations your Excellency.

Wilson: Please Father, don't call me like that.

Dominic: No, you are a Minister (He is smiling and trying to remain relaxed. From the ceiling, a large fan is blowing fresh air.)

Wilson: You know, this thing just happened just like that.

Dominic: I know, this is a Revolution.

Wilson: Yes, Revolution brother (Responding slowly.)

Dominic: What are you going to do now?

Wilson: Not about our problem?

Dominic: Yes.

Wilson: Yes, of course federalism is very very important (He is breathing heavily and sounding like important.)

Dominic: We shall rely on you, and on His Excellency Gatluak.

Wilson: Of course. By the way His Excellency Gatluak

sends you his best wishes.

Dominic: Me too. Please do not forget our…

Wilson: Of course, brother, of course (Pressing his hair backward slowly.)

Dominic: How is Lupai, have you seen him Your Excellency?

Wilson: Lupai, I haven't seen him since (He is breathing heavily, and the hand is still on the hair.)

Dominic: Okay, is Mrs. Dudu here, I want to greet her.

Wilson: Oh yes, of course.

Minister Wilson Andrago got up slowly and started to walk slowly towards the inner part of his new ministerial mansion, and Dominic observed his friend. He was walking in some heavily measured strides with arms apart from his body, "Did he use to walk like that!" Father Dominic wondered. The Minister came back slowly and sat down slowly, looked around slowly, breathed slowly but heavily. He is looking important. Soon Mrs. Dudu appeared, and she greeted Father Dominic warmly and tried to shy away.

Dominic: My congratulations Dudu. I have come to greet you (Mrs. Dudu is hiding her smiles by casting her head down.) Dominic assured her of his happiness for their new house and life, and that may God bless them. He told her that he is going to miss her delicious food.

Mrs. Dudu: No, no Father, you are welcome, I will cook the food you like.

Dominic: If my friend Wilson can invite me, I will come.

Wilson: No, brother I mean Father of course, you are welcome any time, any time, this is your house Father (Sounding friendly and small laughter.)

As Wilson completed his sentence, Esther entered with a tray in hand with tea and all kinds of sweets in it, and Winston toddling behind. Wilson quickly got up to help the little girl who now appears shining, why not; she is now a daughter of a minister, and she should reflect all that. Presently, Mrs. Dudu got up and cooperated with this shining girl to prepare tea for the Father.

Winston wedged between his legs, Wilson looked somber and important like some newly appointed ministers sometimes would do. Over the cup of tea, Dominic's mind and conscience are bogged down; should he be jubilant because his friend has just been appointed minister, why? Is he disappointed because his dear friend might be implicated in this undemocratic system, and that this may smear his good name no matter what good intentions he may have, why? Or should he be angry because his friend is beginning to behave in an awkward manner, a behavior that might undermine his image in the future, why should he? But definitely he is not happy. He is not feeling comfortable with the way his friend behaved today, a feeling he shared with Father Saturnino.

Nevertheless, Father Dominic began to feel that developments were fast forward moving. A few days ago, he did not contemplate that two of his close associates could become ministers in this new Arab Revolutionary Government. But who knows, these two gentlemen may make a difference and may convince the North to implement federalism.

Moreover, news reached him that Father Saturnino had suddenly left the country, and that he is not coming back again as long as the Arabs continued to refuse to grant the South the right to federalism, the right it undoubtedly possesses as a consequence of the principle of free self-determination which reason and democracy grant to a free people.

Not long however, than the new Revolutionary Government announced the abolition of Sunday as a day of worship and rest in South Sudan "Why, what is wrong with these people, why abolish Sunday eh?" This issue disturbed the former Member of Parliament and former priest greatly, "How, how can this happen, why do you abolish Sunday in the South, how do you expect us tototo to, to stay together," Father Dominic protested strongly but to whom should he direct his protest under this Revolution? "Well, we shall see," Dominic would school himself.

As a result of the abolition of Sunday as a holiday in South Sudan, Dominic was told that many political activists in the South deserted and some began to form clandestine resistance units in the forest, and that some of them had already gone into exile in Kampala and vowed not to return until this policy is reversed.

CHAPTER ELEVEN

Disappointed

Weeks and months soon swept by, and Parliament remained closed, and no source of income for some former Members of Parliament. At last, Father Dominic Muorwel got appointed teacher at Comboni Intermediate School and could reasonably manage his affairs but kept sharp eyes and ears on political developments.

In 1962, the Revolutionary Government passed The Missionary Societies Act that expelled all foreign priests from South Sudan within 48 hours. This rekindled sharp and angry reactions in the soul and mind of Father Dominic. He felt extremely humiliated, "Howhow, how can this happen, why? he fumed. "What is happening, what is happening, nooo, nonono. I am sure those of Gatluak and Wilson will do something to reverse the policy," he assured himself.

The two local Arabic newspapers and the only independent English daily newspaper The Vigilant, run by South Sudanese, began to report increasing rebel activities in the South and those developments revived some hope in the heart of Father Dominic, after all he had foretold that if the North is adamant on refusing an arrangement whereby the South rules itself, the South would opt for an armed struggle; on this all the Black Bloc members agreed, Wilson knowns it and Gatluak knows this.

However, Father Dominic and the remaining members of the former Black Bloc received sad news about the mysterious death of Father Saturnino O'hure Hilange on the Sudan-Uganda border. Sources mentioned that Father Saturnino Hilange, an active rebel leader fighting for the cause of liberation, was killed by Khartoum agents in collaboration with Ugandan security organs, and Father Dominic would go enquiring, "Is this really true, have they killed him, has he died really? Oh God," he was sobbing quietly, "May the Almighty God rest your soul in eternal peace;" and would wipe his tearful eyes clean.

In his search for an assurance that the news may not be true, Father Dominic would visualize his old comrade in Christ; how friendly he was, how courageous he was, how stubborn he was, how noble he was, how committed to the cause of the South he was, how committed a priest he was, how faithful to Christ he was; this tall son of the Latuka homeland, son of the Imatong heights, land of the strong headed, land of the fearless warriors. He refused to resign from priesthood. He died a faithful priest and a faithful nationalist, the former priest was lamenting and praying.

There was many a time Father Dominic Muorwel wished he was with Saturnino, his soul brother, a friend and brother in Christ and a comrade in politics. Dominic earnestly wished he was with Father Saturnino there in the jungle, under those tall trees, under the rains, come what may, carrying guns and fighting alongside; Christ would not object self-defense, would he? "Father Saturnino, wait for me I am coming," Father Dominic would wipe these angry drops from his cheeks and tried to look as composed as possible.

Nevertheless, Dominic saw that the new Revolution vessel was continuing to gather momentum. On its voyage, perilous as it seemed, the vessel continued to move ahead and was ready to drown anybody that stood on its way.

Against all odds and obstacles, the Revolution soon discovered that it enjoyed support from both the masses who were disillusioned in the poor performance of the ousted democratic government, and in many members of the defunct political parties; except Dominic among a few others who, on matters of principle, opted to stay away and preferred to wait for what the two of his former MP colleagues and now ministers may do.

Despite the resolve not to have anything to do with this Revolution, Dominic began to hear disturbing news that some of the former ministers in the recently ousted democratically elected government including some South Sudanese began to flirt with the new system, and that some of the former Members of Parliament started to tender their good services to serve this Revolutionary regime; "How, how can this be, how can one serve a non-democratic government; this is unbecoming, this is undemocratic; this is betrayal," Dominic went about enquiring and protesting.

What pained him the most was the news that one of his close friends and confidants, former MP Lual opted to join this Revolutionary Government, "Oh no, can this really be true, has Lual really joined this system really!!!" And Dominic kept looking for any flimsiest ray of hope that this news was not true, but there it was.

Being a man full of pride and above all a man of principles as he believed, former priest and former MP and now a teacher, Dominic vowed he cannot and will not think to join this or any other government that will not be ready to solve the Problem of the South in the way Southerners want. Nevertheless, the defection of Lual in particular, was a great blow to his conscience, hopes and expectations. But, feeling powerless to change things the way he would like, Dominic conceded to allow Lual and others to try their luck, "who knows, they may do something," he would console himself.

In as much as Dominic was concerned and disappointed at what Lual did, it was reported that Lual, too, was very much disappointed and upset with the negative attitude of Dominic, "Why, why is he angry with me now eh; what he want from me eh, he do not know this is politic; now howohowhow how; what he want me to do; sit like that?" Lual defiantly retorted.

From henceforth, both former MP colleagues and now former friends, seemed to have parted, each angry at the other, one was adamant on what he considered party politics and the other was contended on what he considered practical politics.

Moreover, Dominic learned that many former MPs from various Northern Sudanese political parties had also joined the bandwagon of this new Revolutionary Government, some openly and others discreetly. But why did some Arab politicians from defunct but well-established political parties seek to join this Revolutionary Government, a revolution that has infringed upon democracy. Dominic went about wondering.

Dominic concluded that those politicians either lacked principles, or were power hungry "Look at these politicians, most of them are just opportunists and many of them may lack principles." However, on looking at the matter from another angle, Dominic began to believe that in as much as some politicians lacked principles, opportunists or simply position seekers, this Revolution vessel seemed to be empty and was ready to take anyone on board, "If that is the case, then let them join; it is an empty vessel, anyone can board," thus Dominic convinced himself.

There were times in which the former MP could see some sense in defections than in what seemed to be naked lack of principles which often leads others to be seen to compromise on principles, or simply greedy and self-seeking opportunist. Here in the North, life is so difficult that not any unqualified or any person without a profession can bear for a considerable length of time without bending. A person has to find a way to make a living, no? Or perhaps could it not be him who has failed to understand the rules of the game, or failed to read the signs of time? In simple terms, politics is dynamic, somebody told him. This means that politicians should be practical, and that politics is a profession fit for practical people and not for those who are rigid or so idealistic, or too romantic.

In this respect, Dominic remembered people telling him that David Angundit often thought of him as "just a poor priest who did not know politic," and Celestino Awan was also reported to have said something of the kind about him; could this be true. But this harsh judgment was balanced off by news that came from the South from time to time.

News that reached Dominic Muorwel from the South directly and indirectly often spoke of increased rebel activities. For example, just last week The Vigilant published a news report that rebels occupied a police station and hoisted their flag. To Dominic this was what rebellion is all about; fight face-to-face, defeat the enemy, and take over the station and towns, hold on and establish an administration, in the end there will be a political settlement. Thus, the Vigilant newspaper remained his favorite companion, it kept him fed with good news, and sometimes bad; above all this newspaper kept him informed about the progress of Any-nya military activities in the South. With Anya-nya flame burning, Dominic strongly believed that the Arabs will one day realize that it is better to look for a political settlement.

Two years have quickly passed, "Why is it cold like this, it is October!!" wondered Father Dominic wrapped up in a jacket as he huddled under the veranda late in the evening. However, it is sometimes true that certain dramatic developments may drag feet but never late, and there it was.

Despite the cold weather, the people of Sudan took to the

streets in a popular uprising that ended in what is termed the October 21 Revolution. Mr. David Angundit was once more appointed Minister in the new cabinet alongside Mr. Gatluak Biliu. But surprisingly, former Member of Parliament Mr. Lupai Jada was appointed Minister to represent his Province. Again, Father Dominic's head spun around, "Howhow how what is this; it is very strange," Dominic wondered, "What do Arabs see in these people now eh; Angundit, Gatluak, what did they do to the South; whatwhat, what; well let us see what Lupai can do. I know he is a man of principles."

Soon, Dominic received another blow on the news that Gatluak did join one of the contesting Northern Sudanese political parties, "Oh, no no what is wrong with these people, Gatluak, have you forgotten the problem, did you not vow we will fight; did you not say you will fight? It is strange," Dominic wondered indeed.

In 1965, some Northern political parties pressed that the problem of the South should be solved peacefully and democratically in a Roundtable Conference. Some rebel leaders flew in from East Africa and some flew to Khartoum from Europe to attend the conference to put an end to the problem of the South. Information out from the conference reached Dominic that the Sudan African National Union (SANU) split and both leaders of the two factions sat at the table separately. This issue disturbed Dominic as he saw it a big blow against the hopes of the people in the South, "Is this the time to split, is this the time to split William and you Aggrey; it is time to unite and have one strategy, one voice," Dominic lamented bitterly.

Dominic learned that Northern ideological parties particularly capitalized on this split and managed to abort the resolutions of the Round Table Conference, "What are we going to do, now the Arabs have succeeded to defeat us by causing a split in our Parties; what can we do now; God help us," he lamented.

While the wheel of real life kept turning, Dominic stopped to be preoccupied with what others were doing and began to pay more attention on what he should be doing. Soon a year had passed.

It was Easter season. Dominic Muorwel was walking to church to attend midday High Mass. He was careful as usual by insisting to walk on the extreme edge of the pavement because he did not trust these Arab cars, and therefore, he believed that they don't have any regard for a poor pedestrian like him. As he stopped and looked to the left to make sure there was no traffic danger before crossing, a big black Mercedes Benz passed by. The driver pulled the car to a halt some distance ahead and Dominic doubled his steps to check who was waiting for him.

The passenger wound down the window glass, pulled down his big black goggles and beamed. To Dominic's surprise, here is Minister Lupai Jada in flesh and blood at the back seat. Yes, the blood may have not changed but the flesh has changed, it has become much thicker, brighter, and softer than the time they had their last encounter, this is natural, no?

But the face; oh, the face; thou art mirror some people do not find difficult to mask. Dominic noticed that the mask of His Excellency was bigger, rounder and shimmering, "Look at his eyes, they are twinkling," Dominic remarked silently. Dominic noticed instantly that the eyes of His Excellency have become much larger than they were, and larger they were, the more they revealed so much, "He is a liar," Dominic remarked. Minister Lupai burst into laughter as he extended this thick cold hand to grip this long thin hot hand of his old friend standing under the hot sun.

Dominic: (With some smile and some back bending) It is you Your Excellency Lupai, how are you, sir?

Lupai: (His is coiling at the rear and the voice is big, calm, and confident) I am fine, how about you; long time eh? (A little laughter and this big soft belly would bubble a little.)

Dominic felt the cold fresh wind blowing into his hot rough face as he touched this thick cold hand extending to him, and the cold words coming out from this big cold chest and out from this large cold mouth of his former old friend. Another thing, although His Excellency's English may have not improved much, yet he was using Arabic frequently, and that was not his habit, "You don't look well, what happened, are you sick?"

Dominic: No, no thank God, there is nothing wrong with me, I am fine (Checking himself around with some smile.)

Lupai: I have not heard of you for some time now. How are you?

Dominic: Fine, fine everything is fine.

Dominic felt the distance between them suddenly getting wider as he bent more to reach for those large eyes of the speaker behind this big black car.

Lupai: Where are you going under this hot sun?

Dominic: I am going to church.

Lupai: To church! But it is not Sunday, no?

Dominic: No, it is Good Friday.

Lupai: Good Friday, really, today! Did they announce it on the Radio … or in the TV?

Dominic: I don't know.

Lupai: Wallahi, these people (He is using some Arabic language while wagging into the air and showing a heavy gold ring on his finger) Well, we shall see this in the meeting of the Council of Ministers. But I want to see you, how can I reach you?

Dominic: I am around, just send for me (Some dry smile.)

Lupai: Where are you found?

Dominic: In Comboni.

Lupai: In Comboi, what are you doing in Comboni?

Dominic: I am teaching, what else can I do?

Lupai: No, teaching is good, very good. Okay Father, see you.

Former Member of Parliament and former priest and now former friend continued his journey to the Cathedral shaking his head in disbelief that someone like Minister Lupai Jada did not know that it was Good Friday, "How can this be; the whole world knows that today is Good Friday; who does not know today is Good Friday," Dominic was trying to find an excuse for His Excellency and finally, "Well, that is his problem," Father Dominic shrugged the whole thing off.

CHAPTER TWELVE

No Change

One fine Sunday morning May 25, 1969, the army staged a coup d'état the media called May Revolution. Among the Southerners Dominic knew who got appointed ministers that morning are Minister Lupai Jada and former Member of Parliament Marko, in addition to someone by name Philip Uthuon. Again, Father Dominic's head swirled. He wondered as to the reason that makes Arabs to appoint somebody like Lupai again, "We have seen him before, look at his big stomach, he is laughing all the time; God save us," he would supplicate. "Is he alone, see Marko, what does he know, not only politics, he does not even know how to speak, oh my God. And who is this Uthuon! People are appointed just like that eh, he may not even be a politician," Father Dominic was sickened by the events. He was powerless. He was hopeless and helpless. He prayed to God to save the South.

Friday at the Central Station, Father Dominic Muorwel had just finished eating a sandwich, a cup of tea on the table and was fixing his reading glasses to read the Sudan Standard newspaper that had just been revived. Suddenly, this man stood right in front of him and extended his hand to greet. Father Dominic came to attention and rose to greet the man, "I am Alex, (Father Dominic is holding the hand, the newspaper, and the glass in the other and threw his head up to recall) Alex Suleiman you remember? (Continued the man.) "Aaaah yes, yes Alex," (Interjected Dominic with a big smile) the cousin of Minister Lupai, aaaah yes, yes. How are you Mr. Alex please sit, please sit," (All smiles and showing due interest.)

Alex: Thank you.

Dominic: Welcome. good to see you, sit down Alex.

Alex: (With a big smile) Thank you.

Dominic: Where have you been all these years?

Alex: I have been in Port Sudan.

Dominic: Doing what?

Alex: I am Assistant Attorney there.

Dominic: "That is why I have not seen you for all these years. This is good, very good," 'Exactly yes, exactly,' Alex would respond politely. Dominic continued "That is good, yes, good indeed. welcome"

The two men sat down and prepared to know more about their affairs after all these years.

As he was passing through with a chair in hand, Stanislaus's eyes caught those of Dominic's and immediately the two men warmly embraced, then Father Dominic confirmed that it was the wish of the Lord that made them to meet that day.

Stanislaus: How do you do brother, long time eh? (Big smiles.)

Dominic: Yes, it is a long time. In fact, I was wondering where you have been all these years. How are you?

Stanislaus: I am fine, brother.

Dominic: Do you know this man, Stans?

Stanislaus: (Looking up with these thick glasses) Not so quiet.

Dominic: This is Alex, the cousin of minister Lupai, don't you remember?

Stanislaus: Alex! the cousin of Lupai the minister, I remember (Reaching for his head above the heavy glasses) how do you do Alex, long time eh.

Alex: I am fine; I hope that you are fine (Everybody is smiling big.)

Stanislaus: I am fine. Where are you now, what are you doing?

Alex: I am Assistant Attorney in Port Sudan.

Stanislaus: That is very good, that is very good, yes, very good.

Dominic called the cafeteria attendant and ordered him to bring sandwiches and orange juice for the Assistant Attorney and for the former MP Stanislaus. Alex turned down the sandwich and the juice but settled for a cup of strong tea. Before they could finish this reunion exercise, Mordecai Mabor appeared just in front of them, and this prompted Dominic to repeat the remark he had made earlier that it is the wish of the Lord that has let them to meet here today. And again, Dominic called the cafeteria boy to supply water and tea.

Alex: By the way, I was going to enquire about you, long time I have not seen you.

Dominic: Truly Mordecai, where have you been really?

Mordecai: In El Fasher.

Stanislaus: That is a remote place.

Mordecai: I have just been transferred to El Jeneina.

Stanislaus: That is even farther to the north.

Mordecai: No, to the west.

Dominic: Where?

Mordecai: It is near the border with Chad.

Dominic: Chad! It is truly far.

Stanislaus: I hope now you are a Colonel.

Mordecai: No, I am still a Major.

Stanislaus: A Major; all these years!

Dominic: How many years now?

Mordecai: Well about fourteen years, or something like that.

Stanislaus: Fourteen years, that is a long time, and no promotion! How about your colleagues?

Mordecai: They are all Colonels, some of them are even Brigadiers.

Stanislaus: You see, that is deliberate.

Dominic: That is why we have been fighting for federation.

Stanislaus: Yes, federation was going to solve these problems.

Alex: Who will listen…

The place is getting full of people and songs from the radio are loud. Suddenly, Stanislaus got surprised through those thick glasses and exclaimed "Look, look who is this man," he burst into a loud laughter. "Awan Celestino." All rose to welcome the old brother who is now looking old. Father Dominic must be right on the fact that it was the wish of the Lord that had brought them together in this place today.

After they had warmly embraced and sat down, Dominic enquired about the whereabouts of Celestine who informed them that he had just returned from the South, and that during all those years, he had been doing cross-border trading, and that after all it was not so bad only security problems. Awan informed them that the army threw him in jail and that he was about to lose his life because he was accused of sympathy with the Anya-nya rebels.

Assistant Attorney: Is it really!

Awan: Of course, my brother, go there and see.

Stanislaus: How long did you spend in jail?

Awan: About one and a half years.

Assistant Attorney: One and a half years!

Stanislaus: That is unjust…unjust.

Awan: What can I do. I only thank God I would have finish.

Dominic: I always believe that nothing can solve this problem of ours except fighting.

Alex: Yes, fighting is the only way, yes.

Stanislaus: Because without fighting, these people will not listen to us, you see, yes.

The Officer: You are right.

Although there is some dust hanging in the air and noise in a place like, the former Members of Parliament found this a chance to review the past and to go over certain events and instances involving experiences, ups and downs of politics and particularly the life of the lots of South Sudanese under the different regimes to which Stanislaus confirmed that they have never improved, but rather have become worse.

Celestine: No, not the South! the situation there is bad, very bad.

Father Dominic confided to them that he always believed that the situation in the South will never improve as long as the North denied the South its right to federation.

Right now, under the shade of the Central Station, the assembly of the three former Members of Parliament in the company of this Assistant Attorney and the Police Officer coming from El Jeniena on duty, has uncovered the effect of merciless time and rough life. A close examination reveals that although these men may have not changed in metal, yet they have definitely changed in shape and hope. One can easily notice that white hair is dominating particularly Stanislaus is fast becoming ball headed besides, his eyesight is becoming poorer; look at these heavy glasses.

Look at Celestine. Besides poor sight, ball head, he has lost some teeth probably due to torture and this made Stanislaus about to miss knowing him. However, his general health condition is not so bad to sum it. But these former Members of Parliament see everything around them in sort of a blurred vision; they see faces under the shade here have drastically changed in substance far away from the faces during 1955 when they seemed fresh and lively.

Moreover, the movement of the people has become

slower, besides there are no trams anymore and the radio is not blaring as it used to do and therefore, the situation here is relatively calm. One noticeable thing is that shoeshine boys have remained the same with their eyes ever fixed on shoes as they shuffle along. However, by now the former Members of Parliament have started to mix up the little remaining English with a lot of poor grammarless Arabic language.

Poor Arabic aside, fourteen years of separation seemed to have cleared the heavy clouds of misunderstanding that had once hung-over relations between the former MPs and Celestino Awan who was used to be called the fox. It also seemed that these fourteen years, though not too long, have proven the fact that these former Members of Parliament were in the same boat of marginalization and Awan the fox, the traitor saw this for himself while in the South.

As they sat here heads pooled together discussing the same issues of yesteryears, they felt that they were still comrades fighting for the same cause. But, what about their former colleagues who became ministers in different regimes!

Having treated these issues extensively, Assistant Attorney Alex, opted to turn around by addressing Dominic directly,

"How are things after all these years eh?"

Dominic: I hope you have followed all these ups and downs.

Alex: Yes, very strange very strange (Smile of disbelief and disappointment)

Dominic: Yes, very strange.

Alex: What next; what are you going to do now?

Dominic: Well, let us see what those of Lupai can do.

Alex: Lupai! Are they really going to do something?

Stanislaus: Well, let them try (He adjusts his heavy glasses.)

Dominic: By the way who is this Uthuon…Philip?

Stanislaus: You don't know him!!!

He went on to give more information about Uthuon partly in this broken Arabic and partly in broken English, that he did not have a formal education of any kind, that this Uthuon is very smart, that he is commonly known as diktor (Small laughter.)

Awan: (Small laughter) Diktor!

Dominic: Is he a doctor?

Stans: (In broken Arabic) Doctor what; (In English and some laughter) he is not even educated, just small English here and there, and some Arabic here and there like ours.

Alex: Why call him diktor?

Stans: (Mixture of some Arabic and English and laughter) Actually he is a male nurse; he injects people in the neighborhoods for malaria and for what or what, something like that.

Celestino: He is a male-nurse! (Laughter) a male nurse and they call him diktor!

Stans: Yes, my friend, what can you say.

Alex: (Some laughter) You call a male nurse a doctor!

Stans: They just call him like that what can you say, (Some laughter) but he is smart very very smart I tell you; he can explain any problem, anything, politics whatwhat or whatwhat, even religion (Small laughter) he can explain anything I tell you, there is nothing he cannot talk about, and some people even call him philosopher (Laughter.)

Awan: Philosifer also! (Big smile and some headshaking and laughter.)

Stans: This man, they say he can talk like a philosopher, he speak big big what or what (Big smile.)

The Officer: Philosifer, this man! (Shaking his head and some laughter.)

Alex: (After a while) Have you heard that our brothers in the government have become members of the ruling Sudan Socialist Union?

Dominic: What, Socialist Union!

Awan: How can this happen!

Alex: Yes, you have not heard this? They are all members of the Sudan Socialist Union my friend (Speaking partly in English and partly in this broken Arabic.)

Speaking colloquial Arabic by now has become the order with Southerners, even Father Dominic has now become versant in this simple grammarless Arabic, what can he do; years and real life have taught him to conform but not on principles. Some of his friends recall that Father Dominic thought that Arabic was very strange and difficult, it is written in the opposite direction, just like driving a vehicle against the traffic laws.

Dominic: Unbelievable; how can this happen, Sudan Socialist Union their new Party!

Alex: Yes, those of Lupai and, and this and and, and that all are members of the Sudan Socialist Union.

Stanislaus: My friend, if you are not a Socialist you cannot become a minister, not only that, you cannot even become a messenger leave alone a minister (Small laughter and he is joined by the others while adjusting his heavy glasses.)

Celestino: Is this the case now, I am really surprise!

Alex: Yes, my friend.

CHAPTER THIRTEEN

Goodbye

Days and weeks kept passing by and Dominic seemed more adamant on his principles than ever. In the meantime, news trickling from the South spoke of increase in rebel activities. But surprisingly Dominic was told that Minister Lupai had publicly condemned the Anya-nya calling them outlaws and issued a statement appealing to the rebels to lay down arms and come to the negotiating table, "What, Lupai, you call Anya-nya outlaws, and they lay down arms, you, you!"

It was not Lupai alone who had changed so much as to call Anya-nya freedom fighters out laws. In fact, since revolutions began, Dominic continued to receive disturbing news and sometimes saw with his own eyes people he knew and those he did not, change their political creed as easily as changing one's shirts; people who opted to join this or that Party or system for any reason issued scorching statements against their former Political Parties and even against democracy, "What are these people talking about, are they aware really?" Dominic would go about wondering.

Among the most painful blows former priest and former MP received of late was the reaction from Wilson Andrago on joining Sudan Socialist Union, and Wilson replied angrily, "What does this man want me to do eh, this is the Party of the government." Former priest and former MP could not reply and the best he could do was to bid farewell to his former best friend and wished him good luck.

Dominic was not just a former priest or a former MP, he was a politician, but what kind of a politician was he? Since that time Dominic became more emerged in analyzing this very strange phenomenon involving the issue of change in political principles, and he came to understand that in as much as politics is a dirty game, it is dynamic, and that in as much as some people are egoistically inward looking, many people have urgent basic needs, and no one should blame them. Furthermore, Dominic understood that politics does not tolerate any vacuum; someone must fill it. And so, Dominic kept watching the colorful political stage changing.

As a result, politicians kept changing seats, and some politicians in former political parties kept renewing their lease and joined in, while lucky ones got appointed ministers or would be contended with any post in this government or wait for their turn in the next cabinet; after all it is a game similar to the musical chairs. However, some impatient politicians would cross party lines and become members of this or that Party especially under a Revolution or democracy.

Watching this game tends to make Dominic sick and dizzy and he concluded that politics is indeed a dirty game, and that the church was right when it instructs, "do not mix politics with religion."

And therefore, Father Dominic found himself in the vicious circle of these contradicting positions for he couldn't believe that one of his former best friends, someone with whom he had been in the Black Bloc just fourteen years ago or so, has suddenly joined this Revolution, "What did we agree upon, what did we agree on. Did we not agree to fight, have you forgotten Marko; Marko have you forgotten also, did we not agree that we shall fight; is this the way to solve our problem, where is federalism, Marko eh?

Under those ever-changing circumstances, Father Dominic became sort of confused and needed to understand what makes people change their creed once in power, "Why is it called power, why are you afraid Lupai, Marko eh; why are you afraid; I don't care whether you are Socialist or not, I don't care. No, this cannot be, it is too much. Something must be done." Indeed, it was too much. As a result, Dominic became convinced beyond doubt that things were really bad, and that something must be done.

In the course of doing something, Father Dominic Muorwel began to scale down the number of the members of his household by sending many of them home including his two sisters and arranged an accommodation for Lazarus who was now at high school, "He will be alright," he assured himself.

In Kampala, former priest and former MP realized

that he was being followed by the Ugandan security allied with Sudan as he was also being sought after by different Freedom Fighter movement groups and factions. In line with his political convictions and revolutionary inclinations, Dominic opted to join Sudan African Liberation Front under Lago and was appointed Secretary of Foreign Relations in the Political Office.

In the jungle, Dominic soon discovered that he was deep in the atmosphere of "a revolutionary struggle," and deep in the kind of a revolution mud he might have not visualized while in Khartoum. As a result, sooner rather than later, former priest and former MP found himself engulfed in a series of squabbles and some serious inter-revolutionary confrontations. In the jungle, he saw real revolutionary leaders in action. Each faction leader stood firm on his convictions and on what he thought was the right way to do things. And soon, Dominic felt that he was about to get himself entangled in endless squabbles involving inter-Fronts bloody confrontations.

There was a split in the ranks of the Sudan African Liberation Front and Dominic soon discovered that there were splits everywhere, and that some leaders spent more time in attempts to reconcile differences than in actual confrontation with the enemy. Dominic began to question the situation and was getting fidgety, "What is happening, this is not the way to fight the enemy, you can't fight while divided." Dominic discovered that "divided" was the rule not the exception in the rank and file of some political groups, and in different Anya-nya affiliated camps. In one camp a fight would suddenly erupt between and among rivaling commanders, and this fight often would end up with one camp being overrun by the other, "Nooo, nono this can't be," Dominic began to protest and to express dissatisfaction. Nevertheless, revolutionary Dominic held on.

A born revolutionary, Dominic did not allow himself to be dismayed by or dragged into splits which were going on around him but began to plan how to get out of this situation, "I can't remain here like this," he would keep reminding himself, "I must find a way to get out; this is just waste of time. I want to fight like Father Saturnino did."

Buried in this cloud of revolutionary disappointment governed by squabbles, splits, and sometimes bloody confrontations, and while under those tall trees, under the rains, during the night or day, disappointed as he would say, there were times in which the Padre wished he was in Rome or Milano or Verona; oh Verona, Verona, home of spirituality and serenity and calm atmosphere. In Verona, seminarian Domenico saw the photos of this former slave girl called Josephine Bakhita from Al Goz village in Jebel Mara in Darfur; and he was told how she was brought to Omdurman a slave while she was very small and was bought by the Italian Consul, and learned how she became a nun in Italy, and how she died in Italy in 1949; and about Father Daniel Deng Surur from Abyei; how he was snatched by Arab slave abductors in Gong-Mou on River Kiir, and how he was brought to El Obeid and up to Cairo as a slave boy, and how he was emancipated and ordained priest in Cairo and died in Italy in 1945. Never mind, dismayed Dominic would wish he was with his Italian friends.

Dominic recalled how he insisted to come home to fulfil his vocation; "Look at me here, mama-mia mama-mia alora; these people are difficult to conform, difficult to understand. I say let us concentrate on fighting, only fighting positions will come later, they don't listen. May I not be in the wrong jungle, or may be with the wrong people?"

Dominic began to express doubts and disappointment and he was getting frustrated and disgruntled.

One day disgruntled Father Dominic Muorwel reached Leopoldville and from there he found his way to Brazzaville and off to the Central African Republic. In the Central African Republic, he soon found out again that he was in the wrong country and probably among the wrong people; "I want to fight, where are the weapons?" Father Dominic enquired but from whom. Those he met here were some disgruntled Italian priests who were expelled from South Sudan in 1962 and they were here to render some pastoral services to the refugees, and to help provide them with rudimentary education and simple means of subsistence.

Nevertheless, Padre Dominic felt that some revolutionary blood was still running in his veins. He would spend nights trying to figure out how to open the western front but where are the weapons? He still wanted to fight; "even with these boys and these few men, we could start," He would console himself. How many a time he wondered, "How did Father Saturnino start the Southern front? Where did he get weapons, but why are they not supplying me with weapons, why eh? I have been to that

Embassy even to the Israeli Embassy, nothing, nothing at all." Father Dominic kept asking questions upon questions but without answers.

Not long, Father Dominic discovered a number of hard facts he may have not anticipated. He found out that the Central African Republic was undergoing political upheavals not far from those he had left behind. Just recently the army staged a violent coup and deposed the president and fear was everywhere. And he recalled how the Ghanaian President Kwame Nkrumah was deposed by the military just a few years ago and how the Ugandan Prime Minister Milton Obote was deposed by the army. And before he could settle, news came that the Ethiopian Emperor was deposed, humiliated, and killed, "Oh, come on what is going on; it is military, military everywhere."

Dominic saw that wherever he turned it was military including Congo Leopoldville, Congo Brazzaville, and Chad, Nigeria, Togo, Cameroon, Ghana, Sudan, Mali and here in the Central African Republic. Recently he heard that former president of the Cameroon Amado Ahijo was thrown into prison wherein he perished. Father Dominic soon concluded that it was not only Sudan, but post-colonial Africa was boiling from within. It seemed to him though that the African soldiers everywhere were all angry and hungry for power.

Then he learned that the Organization of African Union Charter passed in 1963 binds all African countries to maintain their post-colonial boundaries by respecting each other's territorial integrity and not to support rebel movements except the ANC in South Africa and ZANO and ZAPO freedom movements in Rhodesia. Above all Father Dominic Muorwel came to understand that Central African Republic was not an exception, that it was not in a position to jeopardize relations with Sudan; hence it was not able to allow any rebel movement to be launched from its territory against any neighboring country, especially Sudan which they saw as an aggressive neighbor.

Dominic discovered that even if there were some young men who could volunteer to fight with him, there was no foreign power ready to supply weapons. All these facts were burning in his hands, in his head and in his conscience. What, is he a failure, did he not promise to fight for the freedom of the people of South Sudan; is he not in exile, hasn't he looked for assistance?

There were a series of heavy rains, and the weather suddenly became humid. There were a lot of flies and mosquitoes and many other insects. Drinking water became so bad besides poor food.

The night before, as he laid down on his bed trying to cool off this high fever afflicting his body and head, he turned around and his eyes fell on these tall figures in radiant robes; "Dominic, get up," in a soft clear voice, demanded one of the tall figures in radiant robes.

Father Dominic: (He was surprised and smiling and began to rise) Who are you?

Man in Radiant Robes: (Smiling tenderly) I am Saturnino O'hure Hilange. Here is your sister Josephina Bakhita; here is your brother Daniel Deng Surur.

Father Dominic: (Surprised and smiling) Saturnino O'hure Hilange, Bakhita Giuseppina, Daniel! But you have died, all of you have died, not so?

Father Saturnino: (Smiling and happy) We are here in front of you.

Father Dominic: You are happy, you are healthy…you are radiant.

Father Saturnino: Yes (All smiling big.)

Father Dominic: You were fighting.

Father Saturninio: I did my part (The other figures are smiling.)

Father Dominic: Is the Lord happy?

Father Saturnino: The Lord is pleased.

Father Dominic: I want to fight like you did, please help me.

Father Saturnino: You need not to.

Father Dominic: Why?

Father Saturnino: Do not worry, they shall have what they want.

Father Dominic: I'm tired.

Father Saturnino: Give me your hand (All of them are smiles.)

News transpired about the passing away of Padre Domenico Muorwel Malow, former priest, former Member of Parliament, former teacher, former freedom fighter.

Did you hear that Wilson Andrago, Gatluak and Lupai, did you hear Marko, Stanislaus, and Lual? Did you hear the news? And you Awan, Celestine Awan did you get the news? Your great brother and good friend, your Father and colleague, former Member of Parliament, your countryman, lover of the land, former preacher of the word of God and former freedom fighter in heart and soul, has gone. Did you hear his angry voice? Have you understood the lesson? Do you still remember him; will you continue to remember him? Lazarus, your uncle, and mentor has left for good. He left to fight for you. Do you remember him? Shall you remember him?

www.ingramcontent.com/pod-product-compliance
Lightning Source LLC
Chambersburg PA
CBHW021357290426
44108CB00010B/281